I am Special

of related interest

Asperger's Syndrome
A Guide for Parents and Professionals
Tony Attwood
ISBN 1 85302 557 1

Pretending to be Normal
Living with Asperger's Syndrome
Liane Holliday Willey
Foreword by Tony Attwood
ISBN 1 85302 749 9

Children with Autism, 2nd edition
Diagnosis and Intervention to Meet Their Needs
Colwyn Trevarthen, Kenneth Aitken, Despina Papoudi and Jaqueline Robarts
ISBN 1 85302 555 0

Autism: An Inside-Out Approach
An Innovative Look at the Mechanics of 'Autism'
and Its Developmental 'Cousins'
Donna Williams
ISBN 1 85302 387 6

Parents' Education as Autism Therapists
Applied Behaviour Analysis in Context
Edited by Mickey Keenan, Ken P. Kerr and Karola Dillenburger
Foreword by Professor Bobby Newman
ISBN 1 85302 778 2

Finding Out about Asperger's Syndrome,
High Functioning Autism and PDD
Gunilla Gerland
ISBN 1 85302 840 1

I am Special

Introducing children and young people to their autistic spectrum disorder

Peter Vermeulen

Jessica Kingsley Publishers
London and Philadelphia

Bay Shore

Acknowledgement

The photograph of Hans Asperger on page 150 is reproduced by kind permission of Läkartidningen.

First published in the United Kingdom in 2000 by
Jessica Kingsley Publishers Ltd
116 Pentonville Road,
London N1 9JB, England
and
325 Chestnut Street,
Philadelphia, PA 19106, USA

www.jkp.com

Library of Congress Cataloging in Publication Data

A CIP catalog record for this book is available from the Library of Congress

British Library Cataloguing in Publication Data

A CIP catalogue record for this book is available from the British Library

ISBN 1 85302 916 5

Printed and Bound in Great Britain by
Athenaeum Press, Gateshead, Tyne and Wear

3/5/0

Special notes

This publication includes images from Corel Draw® and Microsoft® Publisher which are protected by the copyright laws of the U.S., Canada and elsewhere. Used under license.

The worksheets in this publication should not be used by anyone who does not have professional knowledge of autistic spectrum disorders and/or qualified training in dealing with people with an autistic spectrum disorder. The author declines all responsibility for any harmful consequences resulting from inappropriate or incorrect use of the worksheets.

Any suggestions for improving or adapting the worksheets contained in this book are very welcome.

The author regrets that he is not in a position to offer opinions, assessments or consultations on individual clients.

Peter Vermeulen
Vlaamse Dienst Autisme
Groot Begijnhof 14
B–9040 Gent (S.A.)
Belgium

Contents

PART 1: THE MANUAL

Introduction

Guidelines to the worksheets

PART 2: THE WORKSHEETS

Introduction

Origins and background

For years, we have been explaining the phenomenon of autism to parents and professionals in the health, education, and social services. Over the past few years, there has been considerable progress in the diagnosis of autistic spectrum disorders in people of average intelligence. These people with autism have themselves started to ask direct and indirect questions about the phenomenon. This recent evolution has created a new challenge for their parents and for professionals: how to explain autism to them?

In 1997, when I was writing *Het Gesloten Boek. Over Autisme en Emoties* (*The Closed Book. On Autism and Emotions*), I decided to take up this challenge. I devoted a whole chapter to the subject. The lectures I gave on the subject attracted a great deal of interest. Both parents and professionals came to me with lots of questions, and they particularly asked for concrete materials or practical manuals. I had described the general outlines and discussed the main points of interest in my book, but they still needed to be worked out in detail and given a practical form.

But parents and professionals were not the only people who came to me with questions. During our 'life skills' courses for adolescents with autism, the participants themselves had started asking questions about their disability and their problems. A number of sessions on the subjects of bullying and criticism, and especially the sessions on relationships, led them to approach the subject of autism itself.

In June 1998, I was charged with a very concrete mission. An Institute, which specialised in young people with autistic spectrum disorders and a below average to above average intelligence, asked the Vlaamse Dienst Autisme (VDA, Flemish Autism Service), the Centre where I work as a lecturer and autism consultant, for advice and support on a new project aimed at informing these young people about their disorder. This was when I developed the first worksheets and sessions.

There were no models I could use as examples, so I had to start from scratch. In these initial stages, however, I did draw inspiration from Carol Gray's work. She had developed something rather similar to what I had in mind, although her method was aimed at younger children and consisted mainly of letting these children draw pictures. She called it: *Pictures of Me.*[1] Although it was quite inspiring, I found the contents and methods not entirely adapted to the needs and questions I encounter among the young people and their parents with whom I come into contact.

During this period, I was asked to give a lecture in Sweden. Someone from the Swedish Organisation for Autism gave me a booklet entitled *Det är Bra att Fråga* ('It is good to ask').[2] In this little book, Gunilla Gerland explains Asperger Syndrome to people who have this disorder. It is well done and very informative, but what I had in mind was something that would offer more opportunities to add a personal touch, and that also paid extensive attention to explaining certain concepts, such as 'disability' or 'personality traits', which are necessary to create the framework for explaining autism.

I drew most of my inspiration from the courses organised by De Brug (The Bridge), a training organisation for adults with an autistic spectrum disorder. On the basis of more than ten years of experience in training these young people in social skills, we developed specific methods adapted to this specific target group.

In the autumn of 1998, I tested *I am Special* for the first time, with a group of seven young people with autistic spectrum disorders aged between 16 and 21 and ranging from a mild intellectual disability to normal intelligence. Six group sessions of an hour and a half each were organised. This turned out to be too short. In early 1999, a new series of sessions was held, this time comprising eight sessions, with six young people between 13 and 18 and of normal intelligence.

Because *I am Special* was meant both for individual use and for use in groups, we also gave out a copy of the draft workbook to be tested in the context of individual psychological support and psychotherapy. In another Institute, *I am Special* was used in weekly sessions (of approximately one hour each) with three young people aged between 12 and 16.

1　This work method is described in the magazine of the National Autistic Society (*Communication*, Winter 1997, pp.22–25).

2　Gunilla Gerland (1997) *Det är Bra att Fråga. Om Asperger syndrom och högnfungerande autism.* Stockholm, Cura. The English translation *Finding Out About Asperger Syndrome, High-Functioning Autism and PDD.* First published in 2000 by Jessica Kingsley Publishers.

In the summer of 1999, the section on individual differences in appearance and personality was used as part of a De Brug course. Twenty adults aged between 18 and 42, with intellectual levels varying from mild intellectual disability to high intelligence, worked with a part of the workbook. To help us determine the minimum developmental age for using this workbook, I also had the workbook tested by two normally developing children, one ten years old, the other twelve.

Based on these try-outs, we finalised the worksheets and completed the guidelines.

Further development of the workbook 'I am Special'

I am Special is not finished. It will never be finished. It is a workbook, which can only attain its final form and contents through working with it. Explaining an autistic spectrum disorder is a process that requires an interaction with the person with autism in question. *I am Special* is, in fact, more of a process than a product. It is interactive.

But there is another sense in which *I am Special* is not yet finished. The workbook that is now in front of you is the result of two years of work. The try-outs have proved that its current form is useful, both for individual use and for group sessions. However, there have only been a limited number of try-outs. This was pioneering work. Although we have already incorporated some of the users' suggestions on improvements and additions, many more suggestions could still be made, e.g. guidelines for adjusting the exercises so that they can be used with children of a younger development age.

Up until now, there has not been a systematic study of the effects of the workbook. *I am Special* has already been used with many children and adolescents in Flanders. The experiences have been positive, but we have not had much more than anecdotal feedback. Undoubtedly, adaptations are necessary for certain children and young people.

That is why we would like to continue developing and refining *I am Special* with the help of suggestions from people who have used this workbook, whether professionals in the health, education and social services, people with autism, or parents. For this purpose, we have included a page for you to write down any suggestions or experiences. We want to collect all these suggestions and use them as a basis for adapting the workbook to make it useful for the largest possible target group. In this way, *I am Special* will truly become a workbook by and for practice.

Important notes

I am Special is not a treatment or a therapeutic method for people with autism. The workbook is best used only as a part of a more general guidance plan. It is a tool that can be used only within a much broader range of assistance and guidance.

The objective of the workbook is limited. *I am Special* is meant only as a tool for giving information on autism and is therefore often only the start of a much broader process of psychological or psycho-therapeutic guidance. Before starting with the workbook, it is necessary to provide for follow-up. With *I am Special*, we give the person with an autistic spectrum disorder information. This is not without consequences: the person with autism will have to process this information, both cognitively and emotionally. That can be quite difficult. Before offering *I am Special*, it is best to draw up a plan for giving further support to the person with autism after the sessions to help him or her to cope with the new information. *I am Special* opens up a door that cannot be closed again afterwards.

It is best not to start working with *I am Special* without due consideration and planning. A number of important requirements must be met before starting the workbook. We have described these in the guidelines. We strongly advise reading through these guidelines carefully before starting with the worksheets. We also recommend a meeting with all the persons in the network around the person with autism, to discuss the indications and the contra-indications. Together with the parents and other people involved, the following matters should be discussed:

- ° Why do we want to inform the person with autism about autism?

- ° What do we expect from these sessions?

- ° Which negative consequences should we be prepared for?

- ° Who will work through *I am Special* with the person with autism?

- ° How will we treat the questions that arise in the person with autism during and in between the sessions?

- ° How will we organise the follow-up?

Copying the workbook

This workbook is designed to be used. The person with autism is meant to write on the worksheets. Therefore, if no copies are made, this workbook can only be used once. If the workbook is to be used for several persons, the worksheets can be copied. However, copying is *only* authorised for immediate use by persons with an autistic spectrum disorder. Any copying or duplicating of worksheets by any means whatsoever for any other purposes is subject to the explicit permission of the publisher. This permission to make copies of *I am Special* applies only to the worksheets and not to the manual. The pages of the manual are protected by copyright.

Education and training

A workbook is often a great help for the user. However, there is always a world of difference between words on paper and real life. Anyone who starts to work with *I am Special* is bound to encounter problems or situations that are not dealt with in the workbook. No landscape ever looks like the map that represents it…

That is why the Centrum voor Concrete Communicatie[3] organises workshops on *I am Special*. In these workshops, the workbook is explained in a very concrete way. The hands-on, experience-oriented demonstrations and exercises introduce the participants to the methods that lie at the basis of the workbook.

Organisations and professionals in the health, education and social services who want to include *I am Special* in their range of services or want to start a project to give psychological guidance or psychotherapy to persons with autism can turn to the Centrum voor Concrete Communicatie for support, advice, and guidance. Trained experts with practical experience will help them to establish the form and contents of their project, geared to the wishes of the requesting organisation.

---

3 Centre for Concrete Communication, Groot Begijnhof 14, B-9040 Gent (Belgium). Telephone: +32 9 2188388, e-mail ccc@autisme-vl.be

They are special

I am Special would not have been possible without the inspiring contributions of many people.

I especially want to thank Sylvie Carette, Lisbet Van Gijzeghem, Lies Delameilleure, and Christel Van Bouwel for the many suggestions they came up with after testing the first drafts of the workbook.

I also want to thank all the persons with autism who were involved in these try-outs for their input. This workbook was, after all, developed for them, and they were the real testers. Their reactions were invaluable for refining the contents.

Special thanks go to Det Dekeukeleire. With her long-standing experience with people with autism and her collaboration on one of the try-outs, she not only greatly contributed to the contents of the workbook, but she also managed to reshape the first and rather chaotic worksheet drafts into a much more attractive – and, especially, more autism-friendly – instrument.

Finally, I want to thank the publisher, Jessica Kingsley, for her willingness to make what was originally a modest Flemish production available to a large public.

Thanks to all these people, *I am Special* has become something special.

Introducing people with autism to their disability

Explaining autism to a person with autism

Explaining autism to a person with autism is not an easy task. Autism is a highly complex matter. Not even professionals with years of experience agree on the characteristics of autism. When even experts can sometimes be at a loss on this subject, how are we supposed to explain autism to people with autism, who are so easily confused? It is important not to pass our confusion on to them.

People with autism have a different way of understanding things from us. They often don't understand spoken language adequately, even though they may have very good verbal skills. Trying to *talk* about autism with a person with autism is a bit like trying to show a blind person what blindness is by means of drawings and pictures.

People with autism have particular difficulty understanding abstract concepts. Autism is an abstract concept, as the basic disorder is not visible. It is very hard to concretise autism. But concrete information is precisely what people with autism have such a great need for.

People with autism tend to think in terms of 'either/or', 'black and white'. Even the most carefully phrased qualification is likely to be interpreted as an absolute general statement. For instance, if they are told 'the fact that you have autism doesn't mean that you don't have any strong points', they may take it to mean 'I have autism, and therefore I'll never amount to anything', but they may just as well infer 'I can do everything'.

Just like other disabled people, people with autism try to conceal their disability and compensate for it. This means that we have to be careful when trying to estimate their real comprehension. It is easy to overestimate it and, as a result, talk about things they don't understand.

17

Finally, just like anyone else, people with autism who are told that there is something wrong with them have to cope with assimilating this information. Making them understand their autism requires more than just the one chat. It is a process.

When?

There are various reasons for starting the process of telling a person with autism what it means to have autism.

° When a person with autism obviously has unrealistic expectations about his or her future, and keeps this up for a long time, e.g. 'later on, I'm going to get married, have children, build a nice house and drive a fast car'. In most cases, people with autism are simply not capable of leading a life like that. Only a few rare individuals succeed. Therefore, it is better to prepare them for this, instead of waiting until they become more and more frustrated and depressed.

° When the person with autism is or will soon be regularly exposed to unprotected situations. For instance, when young people are going to have to start using public transport to get to the place where they are taking practical training, or when they start going to the movies or to the pub. Their strange behaviour will elicit reactions from strangers and will cause problems sooner or later. When people with autism know and understand that they are different from others, and in what way, they will be better prepared and will learn to avoid certain situations. Any problems they would still encounter will be easier to talk about. Above all, however, a person with autism who understands the situation is likely to be better at understanding other people's reactions, instead of being surprised at being laughed at or being turned down again and again. In this sense, informing them about autism is a preventive measure.

° When the person with autism is confronted with a difficult situation of any kind. Being bullied, having relational problems, and not being able to find a job are all well-known problems for these people. Discussing these problems and helping them find a solution to them is easier when they know what causes them. For instance, when they know what autism is, it is easier to explain why they will have to settle for working in a sheltered workshop instead of having a regular job, and it won't come as such a surprise to them any more.

○ When the person with autism asks questions like 'What's wrong with me?' 'Why does that lady (the social worker) come here and talk with you about me?' 'How come nobody comes to play with me?' 'Why do my classmates tease me?' All these questions contain a danger of over-interpretation. Because of their different way of attaching meaning to words, it is very possible that people with autism mean something completely different from what you think they mean. In other words, you must always try to detect the question behind their question before answering.

At what age?

There is no fixed age for starting the process. A lot depends upon individual intelligence, past experience, and the way the environment reacts to the person with autism. After all, it is best to let sleeping dogs lie. It is better not to give people with autism more information than they can handle. Both starting too early and starting too late can cause major problems. Trying to tell them too early may make them unnecessarily confused. If they are told too late, their ignorance of their disability will cause frustration.

With children of average or near-average intelligence, preventive preliminary steps can already be taken when they start primary school, by explaining about 'inside' and 'outside' and about being different. However, this requires a minimum developmental age of four years. Understanding that one is different from other children demands skills and insights that children with a lower developmental age do not have, such as the ability to comprehend abstract words, the ability to look back at past events or one's own behaviour, the ability to reflect on oneself, comprehension of cause-and-effect relations, and above all, the ability to look at oneself from a different perspective. In order to understand oneself better, one has to be able to look at oneself through the eyes of the others.

Who?

Explaining autism to a person with autism cannot be done in a single conversation. It is a long-term process, a process of guidance. The person who starts such a process should therefore be able to guarantee sufficient continuity. Moreover, this person should be available to answer the many and sometimes urgent questions of the person with autism.

Parents can often guarantee both continuity and availability. However, it is not recommended that they assume the responsibility for starting this process. Parents are, in the first place, parents, and not therapists. If parents also have to take on the task of informing their child of his or her diagnosis, there is a danger of role confusion. The child should always be able to turn to his parents for support and assistance with dealing with the emotional effects of the bad news. Nobody likes to confide in the wrong person and it is not easy to turn for comfort to the same person who breaks the bad news to you. It is not unthinkable that persons with autism would start to evade their parents once they have tried to convince them of their disability. In addition to role confusion, there is also the danger that people with autism may lose confidence in their parents. Even though the parents themselves may be able to cope with such a double role, people with autism find this extremely difficult. Aside from the negative consequences this would have for the parents, it is, in any case, very confusing for the individual with autism.

On the other hand, this doesn't necessarily mean that the parents cannot play any role at all in their child's process of learning about his or her disability. On the contrary, the parents have an essential role to play in their child's assimilation of the diagnosis, namely, a supportive one. They can contribute to their child's acceptance of her autism as something that has its positive sides too. By showing that they have given autism a place in their lives, parents can help to relieve any guilt, anger or sadness their child may feel about those mysterious differences.

For similar reasons, the same goes for the educators and/or counsellors who work with children with autism on a daily basis. It is better for the children that they do not learn about their autism from them, but from a complete stranger. This person could be the educational therapist or the psychologist of the organisation, but it could also be a counsellor from another group or organisation. A thorough knowledge of autism, sufficient experience with autistic spectrum disorders, and experience of communicating with people with autism are more important than a certificate!

In ideal circumstances, the person with autism should be able to approach this person as a confidant, a personal mentor. Of course, there needs to be a close collaboration between this person and the parents. The parents can help to set the priorities and they should be given timely and adequate information about the process, including regular feedback on what is happening to their child and how he or she is receiving and assimilating the information.

The various stages of the process

Explaining autism to a person with autism must be done in stages. It is no use trying to start by explaining autism. First, the person concerned needs to acquire certain concepts and gain specific insights in order to be able to understand the diagnosis. These are:

- Knowledge of the body, in particular one's own body, both externally and internally.

- A basic knowledge of the functions and operation of the brain (autism is, after all, a brain disorder).

- Understanding the difference between people's 'outsides' and 'insides', and knowing that people are different, both as regards their inner and their outward appearances.

- Understanding the concepts of 'illness', 'disorder' and 'disability'.

Only when the person has gained these insights can we combine them into a sort of conclusion:

> 'You are good at certain things and not so good at other ones. The things that are difficult for you have a name: autism. Autism is a disability, it is not an illness. It is the result of a brain disorder. The brain of people with autism works differently from the brain of people without autism. Because autism has to do with the brain, it is something of your inside. Therefore, it cannot be seen from the outside. But autism is not entirely invisible. People with autism behave and react differently. All people with autism are different. So, you are also different from other people with autism. But you have some things in common with other people with autism too.'

Special attention to self-esteem

Getting across the meaning of autism to people with autism implies more than just factually explaining it. It is more than informing them about themselves. Just as with any other person, this information will stir up thoughts, desires and emotions. In other words, you cannot just tell them. On the contrary, it demands that you take the responsibility for giving the person with autism assistance with any emotional repercussions of the news. We must keep a constant check on the effects of the information on the person's self-esteem. People with autism are very sensitive to criticism and negative remarks. This is not because they cannot take criticism, but because they do not know how to take it, and because they are less capable of being prepared for it than we are. Criticism always comes as a shock to them, and negative remarks seem to come at them out of the blue. They are unable to anticipate this. Talking about their problems or making remarks about things they are not very good at are likely to elicit negative reactions or even denial from them. After all, both are very human reactions to bad news. The person who breaks the bad news needs to be prepared for that.

On the other hand, there is no sense in keeping the truth from them. There is no point in telling them that they are good at something when they are not. It is already difficult enough for people with autism to get a good sense of themselves without making things even more complicated by lying to them. Honesty is the only way. Because of their own very absolute way of thinking, they will really appreciate that.

But we must also be careful not to damage their self-esteem. Talking with people with autism should never lead to frustration. They have to deal with enough stress and frustration as it is. The whole process of telling them about their disability must take place in a positive atmosphere, and certainly end on a positive note, but without awakening any false hopes.

The following tips may help a person with autism to cope with the bad news:

° Plan enough breaks in the sessions, preferably with opportunities for the person with autism to works things off physically.

° Give the information piecemeal, not all in one go.

° Ask them about their favourite pastimes or subjects for conversation.

° Use an adapted style of communication, so that all their attention is focused on the message.

° Give the person with autism enough time to ask questions and make remarks.

° And above all: use your sense of humour! If you tell them about autism with a gloomy and humourless face, you can hardly expect a positive reaction.

An adapted communication style

Naturally, informing people with autism about their autism involves two-way communication. It is well-known that people with autism have problems with communication, and especially with verbal communication. That is why the counsellor or assistant has to make sure that his or her style of communication is adapted to people with autism and takes their particular way of understanding language into account.

People with autism understand the world differently than we do. They often attach different meanings to certain words and concepts. For example, when individuals with autism talk about 'friends', they may mean people who are friendly to them or even simply everyone who smiles at them and says hello. We must not be too quick to interpret their words or to think we have understood what they meant. Because of this danger of misinterpretations (which is further complicated by the fact that they can get lost in them too), we have chosen, in informing people with autism about autism, not to start from their point of view, but from a highly structured whole which we present to them: a workbook.

Remember that the words we use to describe their problems and autism are not simple for them to understand. How do they understand concepts such as 'stereotyped behaviour', 'ritual' and 'social interaction'? Even words that seem simple are sometimes given strange meanings. To avoid these misunderstandings, *I am Special* pays a lot of attention to defining and explaining concepts such as 'disorder', 'disability' and 'communication'. When we are talking with a person with autism, we must constantly check what they have understood. The best way to do that is by regularly asking the person with autism to repeat what has been said in his or her own words.

Talking with people with autism also means keeping a constant eye on the long-term effects. Sometimes, an apparently minor detail can suddenly loom large in the mind of a person with autism. Molehills may become mountains. It is essential to try and see things from their point of view, and always to look ahead. Therefore, the *I am Special* workbook is best used only after extensive consultation with the people close to the person with autism (the parents in the first place) on how it will be followed up in future. People with autism are much slower than we are in assimilating information, especially if it is emotional information. They are also less likely to talk about their emotions spontaneously, and certain questions or remarks about the *I am Special* sessions may not surface for weeks or even months. When they do, though, they will need to be answered, and the person with autism will need support.

Just as in any communication with people with autism, one has to adapt one's use of language when explaining their disability. It is very important to give concrete descriptions and to refer to things they can see. Avoid referring to abstract notions. Talking about emotions may be a delicate matter. However, their feelings will have to be discussed. People with autism do have feelings, but to them, these feelings do not seem concrete and tangible. Experience has shown that talking about feelings too much and for too long only makes them more confused. They get stuck in abstract terms. They get overwhelmed because they are not capable of making the difference between talking about emotions and actually having them. And sometimes they get lost in the sea of words. That is why *I am Special* is a very factual and concrete workbook. In these talks about autism, we start with concrete actions, and only then proceed to feelings. When they are given something to do, they have a starting point for further reference. The best insights and solutions are reached through setting tasks, such as 'write down an example of an aid you use'. Talking about autism, in fact, is *doing* things together instead of just talking about them. I am Special was deliberately not written as a *story* about autism. It is a *work*book.

Just as for communicating with people with autism in general, the golden rule in talking about autism is that you must *visualise* things: convey your message using as many visible means as possible. A simple drawing can be a great help. For example, you could show them a drawing of an unconnected or missing wire to visualise the brain disorder at the basis of autism. Making lists can be a great practical help too. People with autism are very keen on classifying, labelling and listing things. It helps them to see the world as an ordered place. This is the reason why *I am Special* contains all kinds of lists, e.g., lists of things they are good and bad at, or a list of solutions and aids for people with autism.

Even averagely intelligent people with autism have difficulty with verbal communication. Moreover, they find it immensely difficult to order their own thoughts and see them in their proper perspective. To help them with these problems, it is important to make them *write* as much as possible. Writing is much slower than talking. It produces visual feedback and it is a way of communicating that does not require simultaneous attention to the reactions of the person you are communicating with. Experience has shown that people with autism who can write find it much easier to express their feelings and thoughts on paper than in a conversation. For that reason, the *I am Special* workbook places emphasis on writing things down and filling things in.

Conversations with people with autism should have a clear structure and should be directed towards a definite goal, and preferably be conducted according to a set plan. It is best not to let the person with autism decide on the subject, the duration, or the course of the conversation. In the hands of a person with autism, the chances are that it will turn into a never-ending, purposeless and chaotic discussion (because of the associations they make). It will certainly not be very result-oriented. If you are talking with people with autism, you should be directive, but you should also take care to maintain a positive atmosphere. When the person with autism introduces a new topic because of certain concrete associations, this needs to be channelled, e.g. by saying 'We will talk about that later, because we have to finish this first' or 'I will take note of it and we'll come back to it next time'. That is why *I am Special* is a structured whole. It demands a clear direction from the assistant.

Reactions to the diagnosis

Many of the reactions displayed by people with autism when they are told what is wrong with them (such as depression, anger, and denial) are very familiar. Many of these reactions are, after all, simply human, and not particular to people with autism. When they are told about their autism, these people will naturally try to assimilate this news and try and find or devise ways of living with it. But of course, their different way of thinking comes into play here too.

People with autism will start comparing themselves with others, which is a normal reaction. But they also tend to focus on concrete details. Because of that, they will tend to connect autism with concrete behaviour. For example, they may deduce 'People with autism only talk about trains', 'People with autism don't talk to other people', or 'People with autism don't have any friends'. It is essential to show them the diversity in the similarities between different people with autism. For example, you could reply 'That other person always talks about trains, but you always talk about that girlfriend of yours, which is just as stereotyped'.

People of average or higher intelligence with autism try to compensate for their lack of 'feeling' by 'calculating' all sorts of things. For them, autism will be something they want to measure, calculate, and compare. They will ask questions such as 'What is my autism percentage?', 'For how long must you talk about a single subject for it to qualify as stereotyped?' The 'calculators' also consider themselves to be different from other people with autism. Sometimes, they make remarks such as 'My autism is milder', 'I am less autistic, I've only got Asperger Syndrome'. Once again, it is best, in this case, to stress the diversity between people and to try and individualise things, e.g. by asking them 'What do you consider important to know about yourself?' In addition, one can also stress that autism is not a question of more or less, but of difference. In this sense, introducing the term 'autistic spectrum disorder' may help to clarify things.

In a few cases, people with autism will freak out when they realise what is wrong with them. They will then make their disorder into a stereotyped point of interest, a real preoccupation. This danger must be carefully considered before the sessions about autism are started. If autism turns into a stereotyped subject, then it is important to limit the length of the sessions, and, when necessary, to make prior agreements about when, where, for how long and with whom the person with autism can talk about autism. In these cases too, it is the counsellor's responsibility to offer them clarity and guidance, because restraint is really difficult for them.

Sometimes, people with autism use their autism as an excuse when things have gone wrong or to avoid certain things. A frequently heard remark is 'Don't ask me, I'm autistic'. It is therefore best to avoid making a connection between an inability to do a certain thing with autism and having to play yes-or-no games about what is or what is not a consequence of autism. If they are unable to do a certain thing, you could ask them how you could help them to master it. Often, their strategy of using their autism as an excuse is a behaviour that they have copied from others, i.e., a form of echo behaviour. When parents or professionals say things like: 'You can't go out because of your autism' or 'You can't understand this because of your autism', the person with autism will start using the same words or strategy due to his or her echolalia or echopraxia.

That is why it is so important not to view a person with autism as an 'autist', but primarily as a person, an individual with his or her own difficulties and limitations, who is different from others, irrespective of whether those others have autism or not. It is very important to view this person as someone who has many more qualities than just autism. Autism will necessarily be the main subject of the sessions, but sufficient time and attention should be spent on the person's other qualities, such as his or her personality, interests, compensatory behaviour, hiding strategies, abilities and desires.

Many of the reactions mentioned above are really strategies for *coping with their autism and seeing the positive aspects of their disability*. Just like any of us, people with autism are trying to survive and develop positive self-esteem. With the help of these strategies, they try to live their lives and be happy with themselves.

But some people with autism do exactly the opposite and can only think of themselves in terms of failure. For instance, they say 'I'm autistic, I can't do anything right, I'm no good for anything'. Research has shown that high-functioning people with autism in particular develop negative self-esteem. Because they are so intelligent, they are capable of seeing things from a broader perspective. They have a better perception of other people's reactions to them and thoughts about them, and that gives them a better understanding of their own shortcomings. These people often get depressed. This is most likely to happen at the onset of adolescence, when they see their peers begin to do things they cannot do or are not allowed to do, such as driving a car, living on their own, having a girlfriend, etc. Their self-image is based on comparisons of very concrete facts. Therefore, it is important to have them make lists of the things they can do, and not just talk about their shortcomings and limitations. Sometimes, it is a good idea to oblige them to write only about their positive characteristics and not to talk about their problems for a while. Of course, if the depression is protracted (> 3 months) and serious, they need specialised help (psychotherapy and possibly medication).

Finally, keep in mind that autism makes it well-nigh impossible for people with autism to think in any other way than in absolute, straightforward, black-and-white terms. It is rare for a person with autism to develop a realistic self-image. Then again, that is rare for any person. Don't we all entertain a few illusions about ourselves? However, they are a lot less capable of seeing things themselves in a broader perspective. It would be unrealistic of us to expect them to have the same kind of idea of themselves as we have. Not even the workbook *I am Special* can change this. We would therefore warn everyone not to overestimate the effects of this workbook.

I am Special is only the first in a long series of stages that make up the process of helping a person with autism to give their disorder a place in their life.

Getting started with *I am Special*

Target group

I am Special is meant for children, young people and adults with an autistic spectrum disorder.

Both the contents and the form of this workbook require certain skills and abilities on the part of the person with autism. It is impossible to set a strict minimum age limit, but the try-outs have indicated that some of the more difficult parts, such as the one about the brain, require a (verbal) developmental age of about nine to ten years.

Secondly, the goal of the workbook as a whole (to get to know oneself and one's autism better) requires a minimum *social* developmental age of three to four years. The person in question must be capable of thinking about him- or herself (it doesn't really matter whether these thoughts are correct or not) and to understand the difference between the 'inside' and the 'outside' of people.

In principle, this workbook can be used with averagely intelligent children (IQ≥90) of age ten and over, and with young people of below average intelligence (IQ≥70) of age twelve and over.

However, in view of the diversity of the autistic spectrum, and especially the typical disharmonious developmental profile of children and young people with autism, this cannot be a hard-and-fast rule. Certain parts of the workbook, such as the section on 'the outside' and the section on disabilities (except for the concept of disorder!) can be discussed with younger children.

There is no maximum age limit. A try-out with young adults went well. For highly intelligent and older adults, the material will have to be adjusted to their age. However, the assistant's approach and style of communicating is of more importance than the worksheets themselves.

Conditions and indications

General indication

Using the workbook *I am Special* is recommended from the moment a person with an autistic spectrum disorder or people in his or her surroundings expresses a need for more information on this disability.

The chapters 'I am unique' and 'My body' can be used before this need arises, by way of preparation for later sessions on autism and disabilities. However, if there is too much time between the sessions, the effect of the structure of the worksheets may be lost.

General criteria

The child must already have the following skills and abilities:

- ° the ability to maintain some degree of task focus

- ° adequate reading and writing skills (if writing is difficult, the assistant can help or can write things down for the child)

- ° the ability to think and talk about his or her own body and to reflect on his or her inner self.

Additional conditions for the section on autism

- ° the participant must realise that something is wrong, that he or she is different, even though he or she may not know why

- ° the participant's self-esteem must not be too negative

- ° the participant should be sufficiently motivated to be receptive to the workbook

- ° the parents and carers must be available for following things up and helping the participant assimilate the information – some of the chapters are very confronting

- ° there must be collaboration with the parents.

Collaboration with the parents

Due to the fact that it is hard to set exact indication criteria and conditions, and that, moreover, these can be very different depending on the individual, a close collaboration with the parents is essential, before, during, and after the sessions. If the young person or adult is a resident in an institution, a close collaboration with his or her carers is also required.

Before the sessions

The indications and conditions for using *I am Special* should be discussed with the parents. If the person with autism in question is a child or young person, the parents must give their explicit permission to explain autism to their son or daughter. Once *I am Special* has been started, it is very difficult to stop the process.

Before starting the sessions, the assistant should talk with the parents about their child's diagnosis and find out when it was made, what their child already knows, and what their child's attitude is towards autism. Parents are also an indispensable source of information that can be used in the sessions. They can give concrete examples concerning the triad of impairments. Finally, parents can provide the assistant with essential information on the best ways of communicating with their child, e.g. 'she finds it easier to write things down than to say them'.

During the sessions

The assistant must keep the parents informed of what has been discussed. The participant can be involved in this exchange. The assistant can set the participants the task of showing their parents the worksheets (or some of them) when they get home. Another possibility is to set them tasks that require the parents' assistance, or to ask the participants to give their parents a summary.

In any case, from the start, we should make it clear to the participants that the workbook is their own, but that they should show it to their parents, so that they can learn more about them too…

The parents should also be contacted in between sessions to find out whether their child uses the worksheets at home or not. The assistant can ask 'Does your child talk about the sessions spontaneously? If so, what does he/she say? Does your child enjoy the sessions? Has he/she been more tense, aggressive or depressed since the sessions started?'

After the sessions

Once the child has worked through the workbook, the sessions should be evaluated by the assistant and the parents as soon as possible. In consultation with the parents, concrete arrangements should be made about the follow-up:

  ° If necessary, arrange for an extra question-and-answer session.

- ° Who can the young person go to with further questions? Where and when?

- ° Who can the parents turn to if their child starts displaying behaviour they can't quite place or can't cope with on their own? Where and when?

- ° If necessary, the person with autism should be referred to a professional for psychological guidance.

To get a good idea of the long-term effects, the assistant could arrange to have an evaluation meeting with the parents a couple of weeks or months after the sessions.

Frequency and duration of the sessions

I am Special can easily be adapted to suit the needs and capabilities of the person or persons with autism, the counsellor or assistant, and the other people in their surroundings. The workbook can be used as a whole, but the assistant can also choose to use only certain parts of it. However, the logical structure of the workbook will obviously be lost if only certain parts are used.

I am Special can be worked through in weekly sessions. It is recommended not to have more than two weeks between sessions, so as to avoid having to repeat too much before being able to proceed to the next exercise. To help bridge the gap between sessions, it may be a good idea to give homework, e.g. to have the participants fill in an extra worksheet or reread certain pages. It is important to schedule the sessions wisely. For instance, avoid starting a series just before the summer holidays, because any progress you would have made before the holidays would be lost again after a two-month interval, and you would have to start all over again.

It takes about 10 to 15 hours to work through the whole workbook (without the extra activities), both when used individually and when used in a group. This corresponds to a minimum of eight sessions. It is impossible to specify how many sections should be treated in each session. The assistant should adapt the frequency, number and duration of the sessions to the age and developmental level of the participants. Sections can be repeated as the assistant sees fit. For some participants, this will be necessary.

In order to maintain the participants' attention, motivation, and concentration, it is better not to make the series of sessions too long. If there are more than 15 sessions, there is a risk that the person with autism will lose track of things, get bored, and lose his motivation ('I know that by now!').

Experience has shown that a session, especially for children, should not last any longer than 45 to 60 minutes. If the participants are older, or when working with a group, a session may last up to an hour and a half. However, the assistant should then plan at least one break. It is best to have a short break. If a break lasts too long, the participants may get restless and have difficulties switching from leisure to work.

Another way of alleviating some of the tension of the tasks is to set the participants a few easier and more playful activities relating to the subject. We have given a few tips in the assistant's guidelines for each section of *I am Special*.

Every session should end on a positive note. This can take the form of a snack or a drink, a short game, or a chat about a favourite subject.

Finally, it is important that the person with autism knows about the timing of the sessions beforehand: at what time they start and end, how long they will take, how often there will be such sessions, and break times.

The assistant or counsellor (guidance)

I am Special is best worked through with a person with adequate experience in the field of autism. Preferably, this person should be a stranger to the participant, i.e. someone who does not belong to the participant's everyday world or surroundings. This has the following advantages:

° A stranger often has more authority than a person from one's everyday surroundings.

° The participant will not be troubled by any previous (negative) experiences with the assistant. He or she will have the benefit of a 'blank slate'. The same is true in the opposite sense too: the assistant will find it easier to take a neutral and positive attitude towards the participant.

° Once the assistant and the participants have gained mutual trust, the participants will find it easier to show their feelings, because they do not have to fear being 'punished' later for certain things they said during the sessions.

Engaging a stranger to do this, however, does call for extra attention to the transfer and for close collaboration with the participant's educational environment (parents, educators).

For children or young adults who are residents in a special institution, the assistant can be:

- the psychologist, the psychotherapist or the educational therapist of their own institution or from another institution;

- a mentor, a therapist, a teacher, or an educator who does not belong to the participants' permanent team (e.g. a teacher from another group).

The assistant must have a positive attitude towards people with autism. He or she must have an accepting, directive and empowering style. It is an extra advantage if the assistant has a good sense of perspective as regards the results of the sessions and the effects of his or her actions, so that expectations are not pitched too high. A reasonable use of humour may be a great help to the participant in getting through the most confronting moments.

Location and materials

The sessions should be held in a room where the assistant and the participant will not be disturbed. It is best to use a room that has no other functions, so that the participant will not have inappropriate associations or read un-intended meanings into it. It is best to hold all the sessions in the same room.

A blackboard and extra paper are useful for visualising.

If the break is held in the same room (with a drink, a game, etc.), then it is best to make it visually clear when and where the participants can have this break.

If specific materials are required for a session, these are listed in the corresponding sections of these guidelines.

Group sessions

I am Special can be used individually or in groups. In many cases, it can be very helpful to bring a group of people with autism together to talk about autism. This offers the following advantages and opportunities:

- They see that they are not alone and that others have problems too. This can be very helpful to them, especially for children who go to a regular school and therefore constantly feel the odd one out. It is often a relief for them to know that they are not the only ones who have to cope with difficulties.

○ They learn that autism can take very different forms even though it is still the same disorder. Everybody has difficulties in dealing with other people, but everybody has their specific ways of coping with these difficulties. In a group, it is less of a strain on their imagination to grasp the concept of an 'autistic spectrum': it is visually and concretely present. Many people with autism frequently compare themselves to others. In a group, we give them an opportunity to do so, in a more or less controlled way. In fact, we are then making use of something they would do anyway: comparing themselves to others.

○ Experience has shown that people with autism are very concerned about their fellows, and that they are often capable of giving them good advice on the basis of their own experiences. The disadvantage is that some of their well-meant advice is completely off the mark, due to their incapacity to see things from another perspective. This is where the assistant's role will be greater in a group than in individual sessions. However, even though they may not always understand each other very well, they usually do feel that they are understood by the others.

○ Experience has also shown that participants in group sessions on autism will often accept a confronting statement from another participant which they would not take from a group assistant.

○ For that reason, the assistant may want to guide the group as a whole, or certain members, towards playing the role of a catalyst. In some groups, for instance, there may be an individual who finds it easier than the others to talk openly about certain subjects (out of lack of shame, naiveté, etc.). Such a person can be a great help in opening up the discussion about certain topics. To give an example: during one of the try-out sessions, all the participants admitted to having been bullied after one of them had said that he used to be the victim of frequent bullying; before this conversation, they had all pretended they had never been bullied.

○ Good assistants can be recognised by the way they use the group as a tool, the way they draw on every participant's potential contribution to the dynamics of the group.

° In a group, the assistant is supplied with much more material to work with than in individual sessions. This material can be integrated into the process.

° For participants who claim they have no problems, the assistant can use the social aspects of the group dynamics to help illustrate social or communicational difficulties. As members of a group, which requires skills such as listening to each other, waiting for one's turn to talk, and using suitable means of communication, it is much harder for the participants to hide their difficulties than in the safer, more structured and more artificial situation of an individual session with their mentor, therapist or counsellor.

° In a group, participants can shield themselves from confronting information. A wise assistant can use this: a remark or a comment that is actually meant for one person in particular can be phrased as a general remark for the whole group, for example. This is much less threatening.

° Finally, working in groups is more economical. More participants can be helped in more or less the same time the assistant would otherwise have spent on helping just the one person.

On the other hand, group sessions have their disadvantages and limitations too:

° In a group, there is a chance that the participants may draw overly positive conclusions from their comparisons, even leading them to deny their own problems. ('The others are much more severely disabled than I am.') On the other hand, a positive comparison isn't always bad. It can give them just that little bit of courage they need to improve their self-esteem. ('I'm not too bad after all.')

° Sometimes, bringing people with autism together leads to conflicts. People with autism tend to involuntarily annoy each other and they don't usually mince words when pointing out other people's defects. However, a capable assistant will be able to use this as useful material for the sessions, e.g., as an opportunity to bring up subjects such as differences between people, empathy, etc.

° Of course, such conflicts can be time-consuming and the group assistant may have to talk things out with certain participants after the session.

° A group offers fewer opportunities for individualising and adapting the exercises to the individual participants, and the assistant will not be able to give the participants as much individual attention as he would in person-to-person sessions. There is a risk that one or several participants will monopolise the group. However, proper group guidance and individual follow-up of the sessions will reduce these risks. Working with a group does not rule out individual guidance. An experienced assistant with sufficient knowledge of group work and sufficient experience can create opportunities for individual guidance.

- People with autism are not always good listeners. For that reason, it is a key requirement that the assistant is a good moderator.

- Not every person with autism is suitable for participating in group sessions. (*Please refer to the conditions set out below.*)

Bringing together people with autism to talk about their autism is still in its pioneering stage. It will certainly take a while to collect material on the experiences and to present them in the form of suggestions and strategies. On the whole, the initial experiences have been positive.

The decision of whether to use *I am Special* individually or in a group depends on the problems of the individual with autism, the skills and experiences of the assistant, and a whole series of practical considerations. For instance, it makes a difference whether the participants know each other (e.g. because they are from the same school, class, or group home) or not. When the participants know each other, the history of their respective relationships, conflicts, experiences, and associations will be a part of the group dynamics. This can have advantages as well as disadvantages, which must be carefully considered.

Criteria for participants in group sessions

In addition to the general criteria concerning the use of *I am Special*, people with autism should have the following skills in order to be able to participate in group sessions:

- they must have the support of a mentor, educator, or parent; and this person has to be available to follow things up with them individually, when necessary

- they must have some listening ability

- they must be able to wait for their turn

- and they need to have the courage and ability to say things about themselves in front of a group.

Preparation of the group assistant

The group assistant's preparation should involve:

- consulting with the parents and other parties involved (mentor, teacher, educator, etc.)

- collecting information on the participants' style of communication, style of learning, and group skills (tempo, level of activity, social subtype, etc.)

- collecting information on the diagnoses of the participants, when they were diagnosed, what the participants themselves know about it and what their attitude is towards autism (e.g. whether they are afraid/ashamed of it, whether there is denial or resistance, whether they blame others for their problems, and if yes, who, etc.).

This could be done during an information session for the parents and/or educators to explain the programme and collect all this information.

The group assistant must meet the following requirements:

- a good knowledge of autistic spectrum disorders

- adequate experience with group processes, and in particular in working with people with autism. The many advantages of working with a group of people with autism can only be attained if the group assistant has got a good contact with the group and knows how to use the unique contribution of each participant for the benefit of the group dynamics

- the ability to maintain a good balance between the group dynamics and the need for individualisation

- the ability to practise the Socratic method with a group (see below)

- a great deal of flexibility. A group assistant needs to respond to many more interactions than an individual counsellor. We sometimes say, jokingly, that 'When you start working with a group of people with autism, you know what you've started, but you never know where it will end'. Counsellors who have a great need for control and predictability would do better not to work with a group

- enough control over the group to complete the programme. This requires a measure of directivity. The worst thing that can happen to participants with autism is to have a group assistant who loses control of the sessions.

If a group is composed of people from the same background (e.g. a school, community or institution), it is recommended that there are two people in charge of the sessions. One of them is the actual group assistant, who directs the whole process. Preferably, this is an outsider, a person who does not belong to the group of professionals who work with the children or young people every day. This will help the participants to see the connections between all the professionals who have guidance talks with them. It will also give the group sessions a clearly-defined space in their lives. As we stated above, outsiders are often held in greater esteem and are credited with greater authority by people with autism than their regular carers (or parents). The second person then acts as a group supervisor. This could well be a professional who already knows the participants and who can help them to clarify things.

Even when the group is composed of children who don't know each other, it may still be a good idea to have two people in charge. This offers more opportunities for individualising or for giving participants extra back-up or help with certain tasks.

The difference between the roles of these two people should be very clear. We recommend that they do not constantly and unexpectedly switch roles (i.e. the assistant should not act as a supervisor, nor should the supervisor take charge of the group). This would be too confusing for the participants, e.g. they will not know who to go to if they want to say or ask something. Therefore, the two different roles need to be strictly defined. To continue with our example, when a participant approaches the supervisor with something that needs to be communicated to the group, the supervisor should tell this participant to ask the group assistant. In order to avoid the 'splitting' phenomenon, in which one person is attributed with all the good characteristics and the other with all the bad ones, good communication between the assistant and the supervisor is a must.

Selection, composition and size of the group

Ideally, a group should comprise five to eight participants. The participants should be selected according to the criteria listed above. In an ideal group, there should be a good balance between heterogeneity and homogeneity. To ensure a good group dynamic (and with a view to explaining the autistic spectrum), it is best not to have too many participants with similar characteristics. It is obvious that a group composed of mostly passive, shy, and withdrawn participants, for instance, won't be very energetic. Conversely, if the entire group is made up of active-but-odd types, you will get too much energy for the sessions to be effective. On the other hand, we recommend that participants are selected who are not too different as regards their age, learning ability and verbal skills. In short, it is best to go for heterogeneity of the autistic spectrum within a certain homogeneity of age, intelligence and level of activity.

To avoid having the sessions end in chaos because there are six participants with an Attention Deficit and Hyperactivity Disorder, it is important to collect information on any extra disorders or syndromes beforehand. Another thing to avoid is a group in which all the participants have very low self-esteem or a particularly negative attitude towards autism.

Next, there is the question of whether the participants should ideally already know each other or not. Both have their advantages and disadvantages. When they don't know each other, the assistant will have to spend some time and attention on building the group in the beginning. The structure of *I am Special* provides for this. The exercises on the worksheets 'my outer self' and 'my inner self' are an excellent introduction. For participants who have not met before, this way of offering predictability and clarity will help them feel more secure.

When the participants already know each other, the existing relationships and associations should be taken into account when composing the group, as they will certainly come into play during the sessions. For example, the session on 'my weaker side' may not work for one participant because he has been put in the same group with a person who bullies him. There must be a preponderance of positive relations in the group.

The concrete location of the participants is very important too. Participants who are prone to distraction are better not placed with their face to a window. It is often necessary to make participants change places after the first or second session. If two participants tend to stick together, it is best to separate them. Individuals who generally need special attention can sit next to the group assistant.

Making clear agreements beforehand

Because of their difficulties with social interaction, participants with an autistic spectrum disorder sometimes lack certain skills for participating in group discussions. For them, and for the group assistant, setting clear rules for the sessions is a great help. Here are some examples of rules that could be set:

- ° We listen to each other.
- ° We let the others finish their sentences.
- ° We raise our hand if we want to ask or say something.

- ° We don't touch other people.

- ° We don't criticise anyone.

- ° We write down any questions that come up during the week or ask our parents to write them down for us.

These rules can be made visually present by writing them on the blackboard or on a large notice.

Introduction to the person with autism

First, we set the objective: to get to know yourself and your autism in a better way.

The assistant starts by explaining that *I am Special* is, in the first place, meant for the participants themselves. It will help them get to know themselves much better. The workbook will be the person with autism's own personal workbook. It is like a book that he or she will help to write. It doesn't have to be handed in. If the participants want to, they can always read parts of the workbook again after the session.

The workbook, or parts of it, can also be used to introduce others to the person with autism. Very often, when a new school, a new group home or a camp is contacted, it is the parents who supply information on their child. Not all children and young people with autism like that, but at the same time it is very difficult for them to talk about themselves. We explain that their workbook will make it easier for them to introduce themselves. By letting a person read the workbook, they will be able to communicate key information about themselves without having to engage in direct verbal communication.

We must state clearly that *I am Special* will not tell them everything there is to know about autism and about themselves. A number of children and young people with autism may think something along the lines of 'let's finish this quickly, so I can get my "autism certificate" and know everything about it'. That is why we must tell them that they will learn a lot by working through the *I am Special* book, but that 'getting to know oneself' is a process that is never finished. The same goes for getting to know and understand autism. We also tell them that *I am Special* will supply them with information, but that that is not the end of it. They will have to do something with that information in their lives. They will have to use and apply that knowledge in real life. In other words: *I am Special* is only a beginning.

Overview of the themes

People with autism set great store by predictability. That is why the assistant should offer them an overview of the themes that will be treated in *I am Special* from the beginning.

Some participants expect that even the very first session will be about autism. That is why the point of the first sessions needs to be explained. If we do not do that, they will not understand why the session looks at different things, e.g., to the subject of the brain instead of autism, and there is a risk that they will lose interest.

To motivate the sessions prior to the actual part about autism, it is best to use an image that symbolises a structure, e.g. that of a house. The assistant could draw a picture of a house and thereby visualise the structure of *I am Special*. It can be explained further that the sessions on the body, inside and outside, and other disabilities, are the necessary foundations on which to build the knowledge about autism.

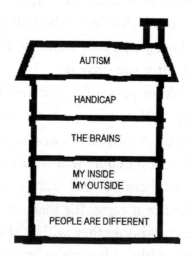

Another image that could appeal to people with autism is that of the alphabet. The assistant can tell them that the first sessions are the letters with which they will be able to read, write, and understand the story of autism.

Moreover, it is recommended that a summary of the remaining parts is given at the beginning of each section. The workbook contains tables of contents.

Giving the workbook a place

By 'giving the workbook a place', we mean explaining the workbook and the sessions in such a way that the person with autism can give them a place in his or her life. People with autism have difficulty with connecting things and we need to help them connect the *I am Special* workbook with their everyday life.

In the first place, we do this by giving them an overview, not only of the contents but also of the frequency, duration, and place of the meetings or sessions. This gives them clear-cut answers to their questions of what, when, how often and how long. Secondly, we also give them clear information on the people who are involved. That is more than simply telling them who is going to conduct the sessions. It is desirable to also provide answers to questions such as 'who can, may or must look in my workbook?', 'who can I talk to about it?', 'who can I go to with questions about the workbook or its contents?' The involvement of the parents and/or carers should also be clarified. If a young person has a network of persons who have regular conversations with him or her, such as an assistant, an educator, a mentor, or a psychologist, then '*I am Special* should also be given a place in that guidance network.

Depending on their experiences and expectations, the participants will attach a certain meaning to the *I am Special* sessions. If they are group sessions, some will identify them as a form of social skills training. Depending on their previous experiences with this kind of training, they will have positive or negative associations. Some young people and adults may experience the sessions as classroom lessons, especially the ones about the body. If the sessions are individual, they should be inserted in the overall context of educational and therapeutic sessions.

Page numbering

I am Special is designed for flexible and individualised use. The choice not to number the worksheets is deliberate, as it allows to add, omit, or replace worksheets at will, without running the risk of confusion among the participants 'because the page numbers aren't right'.

However, there is enough room to number the pages. The assistant can do this or can have the participants do it themselves.

Moving, omitting, or adding worksheets

The worksheets are presented in a logical sequence, according to the structure described in the section on the theoretical background. However, the assistant is free to change the sequence, leave bits out, or add elements.

The worksheets about the outside of the body may, for instance, be used directly after the first worksheets about the outside of the person, before proceeding to the inside (see the worksheets on personality, etc.).

Although, for certain individuals, and certainly for adolescents and adults, it may seem feasible and desirable to skip certain parts of the workbook, e.g. those on the body, we would advise not deciding to do this too quickly. Most of the participants will have learned about the human body at school, but their knowledge may no longer be ready or accurate. A brief refresher will do no harm. For the participants, it will revive their memory of the subject, and for the assistant, it will indicate how much the participants know and/or realise about themselves. For many younger people, this part is easier, because they will have been taught about the body quite recently, which means this section can be a bit of a break in between the other worksheets that demand a greater effort.

People with autism, and certainly the more verbal ones, are easily overestimated. We must not suppose that they know certain things or have certain skills without checking that they actually do! The fact that everyone has an inside and an outside, what belongs to the inside and what belongs to the outside, the fact that every person is unique... all this proved to be surprisingly new for a group of normally intelligent adults with autism during a course of our 'life skills' training project. Most of those participants regularly used words such as 'character', 'personality', 'inner self', etc. Before the course, we thought the participants would find the worksheets on outside and inside rather simplistic, but we were wrong. What seemed self-evident to us, was a revelation to them...

For certain parts that are found difficult, the assistant can add a few easy and playful worksheets by way of relaxation. For instance, he can have the participants make a collage on the star signs of the horoscope in the part on the personality, or have them colour a picture of a wheelchair in the section on disabilities.

If any worksheets are omitted, added or moved, the contents page of each section will also need to be adjusted.

Inductive and deductive use of the worksheets

There are two kinds of worksheets:

- Worksheets with little or no text. Most of them are found in the beginning of the workbook, in the parts on the differences between people and on the human body. After a short introduction, these sheets are handed out to the participants to fill them in.

- Worksheets with more text. These sheets mostly contain information which the participants then need to apply to themselves or give examples of. The section about autism consists mainly of worksheets of this type.

For the worksheets of this second type, two methods can be used.

The deductive method: the assistant summarises the information on the worksheet and lets the participant read the sheet. Then, the assistant asks questions about the information or gives additional explanations.

The inductive method: the assistant poses targeted questions, so that the participants gain the knowledge or insight mentioned on the sheet of their own accord. Once they have given all the answers, they are given the worksheet to read, so that they have a summary.

I prefer the second method myself. This is also called the Socratic method. I have described this method in my book *Brain Cheats*. Just like Socrates, the assistant does not provide the answers or the explanation, but he or she does ask the right questions to help the participant find the correct answers. In this way, we can 'induce' knowledge and insight.

The inductive or Socratic method has a number of advantages:

- It is less traditionally schoolish. In particular participants whose experience with schools is not very positive, or who hate 'lessons', are not bothered by it.

- It gives a boost to the participants' self-esteem: they have arrived at the correct conclusions by themselves! The assistant can give many more positive reinforcements with the Socratic method, e.g. 'Well done!', 'Right!' Of course, this means that the assistant must ask the right questions.

- ° It leads to a much more active participation from the participants. The Socratic method increases their involvement.

- ° The assistant's role becomes less that of 'convincing' the participants and 'proving' things, because it is the participants themselves who come up with the information.

Checking the objectives

In the manual, we list the objectives of each section. We recommend checking, after each section, what and how the participants have understood the contents. This can be done in the form of a list of questions (oral or written), a kind of test (but watch out with children and adolescents who are 'allergic' to school!) or, in a group, in the form of a quiz.

By way of illustration, the workbook contains an example: the 'right or wrong?' sheet on autistic spectrum disorders.

In order to be certain of the effect of the sessions, it is not enough to check the participants' understanding at the end of each section and in the sessions themselves. The good memory and the context-specific behaviour of people with autism may lead us to believe wrongly that they know something or have grasped the meaning of something.

It is best for the assistant to pay explicit attention to the transfer. For instance, this can be done by setting the participants the task of telling people about the sessions, e.g. at home, or at another place outside the sessions. However, many children and young people will not do this spontaneously. That is why it is often better to ask the parents to pose questions to check what and how much their son or daughter has understood of the information given in the sessions. It is important to make it clear to the participants from the start that these things will be discussed at home too. Due to the autistic way of thinking (sometimes combined with other motives, such as shame or resistance to the diagnosis), some participants will otherwise want to confine the contents of the workbook strictly and rigidly to the sessions themselves.

Evaluation

For refining the contents and methods of *I am Special*, we would like the participants to evaluate the sessions and the workbook too. An example is provided in the workbook: the evaluation form that was used in the group meetings of the try-outs.

In our experience, an evaluation is best done in writing and in a structured form. In contrast to what some people think, people with autism are quite capable of expressing their opinion and of making sensible and even very apt remarks. This is easiest for them if they are given very targeted questions, and if they are given enough time to order and formulate their thoughts. A structured questionnaire is a bigger help than an informal talk with open-ended questions such as 'What did you think about it?'.

After they have filled in the evaluation forms, the replies can of course be discussed.

Possible effects

The main aim of *I am Special* is to introduce the child, adolescent, or adult to autism and to inform her or him of the disability called autism.

The workbook is only an aid to doing this. In addition to *I am Special*, many other resources will need to be used; in the first place, regular talks with the person with autism. Moreover, the aim of the workbook is informative rather than therapeutic.

No miracles should be expected of *I am Special*. The workbook gives no guarantee that the participant will come to understand the disorder fully. Nor may one expect a young person with autism to come out of the sessions with a realistic self-concept, or with answers to all his or her questions, or that the sessions will expel all doubts or reservations. The workbook is only a step in a life long process of learning to understand oneself, and especially, learning to live with oneself, as a person with autism.

But even with these reservations, the workbook has its value. From experience, we have learned that it may have the following effects:

- The workbook may work as a catalyst, activating or speeding up the process of dealing with the disability.

- The workbook opens up a lot in the participants, more than an ordinary conversation would. That is why the workbook must not be offered without a follow-up. The questions and remarks that arise on account of the workbook must not be left at that.

- *I am Special* may increase the willingness of the child, adolescent, or young adult to accept guidance. The workbook may help the person to understand more fully why he or she goes to a special school, why aids such as schedules are used, why certain things are difficult, etc.

- The workbook may help to give a person with autism a better-balanced self-concept and a better understanding of autism. It is a way of correcting associations, meanings and experiences that were previously very black-and-white, absolute, or distorted by autistic thinking. The workbook may remove a number of misunderstandings.

° It is an ideal instrument for starting psychological or psychotherapeutic help, because that way one gets to know the person better and one is given material to talk about.

° The workbook is ideal for being used as part of social skills training.

Because the information is written down, the workbook is a tool for streamlining communicating about autism and presenting it in an unequivocal way. If everyone around the child, adolescent, or young adult reads the workbook, the same information and the same terminology can be used. This can be a great help, because people with autism easily get confused when different people use different words, even though they mean to say the same things.

Use with other target groups

With a few alterations, the workbook can also be used to explain autism to siblings or classmates of a child or adolescent with autism. In the boxes, the words 'I' and 'mine' can be replaced by 'my brother/sister' and 'his/her'.

We are also thinking of sessions organised in the following contexts:

° a class in mainstream education that has a child or adolescent with autism

° home training

° a youth movement, playground group, or inclusion camp.

Guidelines to the Worksheets

I am unique: My outside

Objectives of these sessions

- To get to know each other: the supervisor and/or assistant and the participant(s).
- To get to know the method of the workbook.
- To identify and name external (bodily) features of oneself.
- To know that all people differ from each other in their outward appearance, but that there are similarities too.
- To be able to name the external differences and similarities of oneself compared to other people.
- To know that every person's appearance is unique.

Procedure and points of interest

First page

Some children won't want to paste their picture on the first page. The assistant can suggest they use a drawing of themselves instead. Another alternative is for them to write a description of themselves. In the box underneath the picture, the participant is to write down his/her name.

My personal details

People with autism prefer concrete and factual information, such as data, numbers, and labels, to more emotive and abstract information. Most participants will find the sheet for filling in personal details easy to complete. Starting off with an easy and concrete sheet to fill in is an extra motivation to tackle the workbook. If a participant does not know all the answers, the sheet can be taken home and completed together with the parents.

My outside

Again, the workbook starts off with concrete, factual, and measurable information. Some people with autism have difficulties with their body scheme. If any participants encounter these problems, the assistant should pay extra attention to this in this sessions, e.g. by first asking them to name or point to the different parts of their body. The drawing of the human body can be of help with that.

Quite a few individuals with autism do not like being touched, especially when it is unpredictable. In this session, care must be taken with touching, especially if the assistant is male and the participant female, or the other way around.

Some people with autism do not like to look in a mirror either. If any participants have this problem, and, for instance, do not know the colour of their hair, somebody else can name it. It is generally known that certain individuals with autism find it difficult to look people in the eye. For that reason, when they are asked to name their eye colour, it is better to use a mirror than to have someone look closely at them.

Examples of 'distinguishing features' to be mentioned on the worksheet are glasses, earrings, a moustache or a beard, freckles, braces, or skin colour.

I look different from other people

This sheet is very useful for groups, because the participants can compare the way they look with the way the others look. They can rely on concrete, physically present examples instead of on their imagination. For many people with autism, it is extremely difficult to make mental comparisons, even when it is about external features. If this sheet is used for an individual session, it can be given as homework, so that the person can do the actual comparing at home.

If certain comparisons are rather delicate, e.g. if the group includes an overweight person who is bullied about his weight, it is better not to include this In the list of features to be compared.

My outside is unique!

There are two possible ways of using the sheets with text and explanations:

° The assistant can use the Socratic method to guide the person to the desired conclusions, and then have him or her read the sheet as a summary.

° Or the participant can be asked to read the sheet first, and the assistant then asks questions or explains further.

In any case, it is important to ask enough questions to check whether the person has understood the text. The term 'unique' is rarely known and will probably need to be explained. *A tip:* have the person look up the meaning of the word in a dictionary.

Some people will need visual back-up to experience the uniqueness of fingerprints. If they don't believe or understand that no-one has the same fingerprint, the assistant can print his next to the person with autism's. When working in a group, everyone's fingerprints can be compared.

Materials

° photograph

° glue

° a pen

° a pair of scales

° a tape measure

° a mirror

° paint and a sponge or an ink pad

° a ring binder

Variations and suggestions for additional activities

° Have the person lie down on a large piece of paper. Draw his or her contours using a pencil or a felt-tip pen. (This results in a life-sized profile.) The various body measurements can be added to this drawing.

This part of the workbook is well-suited to many different group games that are a lot of fun. A few suggestions:

° Have all the participants line up in order of height. Next, in order of weight, shoe size, darkness of hair, etc.

° 'Cat-in-a-corner' First, select two corners of the room. Next, call out a series of attributes that divide the group in two groups, e.g. 'Everyone wearing shorts, go to the corner next to the window; everyone wearing trousers, go to the corner next to the door'. The participants are to run to 'their' corners as quickly as possible.

- 'Who is it?' All the participants write down three of their own external attributes with which they distinguish themselves from the others, e.g. 'I've got a blue jumper on, I'm wearing glasses and I have long blond hair'. All the pieces of paper are then folded and placed together in the middle of the room. In turns, everyone opens a note and says whose it is.

- 'Who is it?' A variation on the previous game. One of the participants leaves the room and the rest of the group chooses who will be 'it'. Then the person may come back and has to guess who 'it' is by means of questions referring to external characteristics (e.g. 'Is it a boy? Does he have black hair? Is he wearing a green shirt?').

- 'What has changed?' One of the participants leaves the room. Now all the others change something about themselves, e.g., they switch shoes or exchange jumpers. When the person comes back in again, he or she has to find out what has changed.

These sessions and the sessions about 'the inner self' can be further documented by all kinds of texts, pictures, drawings, or cartoons about differences between people.

I am unique: My inside

Objectives of these sessions

° To be able to name the various aspects of a person's inner self (in general): interests, nature, abilities.

° To get to know and be able to name one's own interests, characteristics, talents, and shortcomings.

° To realise that, as regards these aspects, all people differ from each other, but that there are similarities too.

° To be able to name the differences and similarities between one's own interests, characteristics and abilities and those of other people.

° To know that everyone's inner self is unique.

° To gain self-knowledge and get an idea of one's own nature.

Procedure and points of interest

In contrast to the part about one's physical appearance, in which things were externally observable and comparable, this part is more difficult because it requires a degree of ability to see things in a invisible perspective, and a measure of self-reflection. We recommend making things as concrete as possible and illustrating everything with telling examples.

My inner self

The information on this sheet can, again, be presented in either a deductive or an inductive way. Deductive: the assistant names the different aspects and explains. Inductive: the assistant asks the person with autism to name all kinds of personal characteristics of him/herself or of other people and to group these on a sheet of paper or on the blackboard. Next, they are to name these groups. If this turns out to be too difficult, the assistant can name them herself.

If you are dealing with intelligent people with autism, who often know a whole lot of theoretical definitions and synonyms, it is best to avoid endless discussions about terms and definitions. Some of them can hold forth at great length on the notions of 'temperament', 'feelings', 'personality' and the differences between them. Instead of losing time on these discussions, agreements can be made about the contents and meanings of the terms used in these sessions.

My interests and preferences

If desired, the participants can also be asked to state the reasons for their preferences. Under each of the themes, they then write 'because:…'. Naming their favourite activities generally seems to be easier for them than explaining why they like them. Intellectually disabled and younger participants will often say something like 'because I think it's nice' or 'because I like to see, eat, read, hear, …it'.

My nature

The participants are to paste (or write) character traits that are applicable to themselves in the boxes on this worksheet. More boxes can be added if necessary.

Because it is quite hard for people with autism to name character traits, two lists of traits are given for them to choose from. It is easier for people with autism to select options from a list.

The first list consists of opposites, such as 'closed' versus 'open'. The second lists character traits without their opposites (the opposites of these qualities are often negative, such as 'dishonest', 'unfriendly', 'antisocial'). Experience has shown that choosing from the second list is harder for people with autism than choosing between two opposites. If anyone has difficulties to name his or her own character traits, they can be asked to choose between two opposites. For instance 'Do you consider yourself to be more funny than serious?' In groups, this session could include a variation on 'Cat-in-a-corner' in which the assistant names two opposite traits and the participants have to decide in which corner they belong.

Note that, although choosing between opposites is easier for them than naming traits out of the blue, people with autism still consider it quite hard to have to choose. Some people with autism tend to avoid this difficulty by giving ambiguous answers: 'I am quite open, but I'm also closed sometimes', 'I am a bit of both'. It can be helpful to add the word 'rather' or to ask directive or prompting questions such as 'Which of these two applies to you most?'

People with low self-esteem or a defensive attitude will tend to choose only positive qualities. Here are some suggestions for dealing with that. Explain that everybody has both positive (nice, pleasant) traits and less positive traits. Tell them that this doesn't matter, as nobody is perfect. In fact, both positive and negative traits can have their advantages and disadvantages. Give examples. For instance, a fearful person is less likely to cause an accident due to rashness, but on the other hand, such a person will never feel the kick of doing something exciting either; a person who is very open is much more vulnerable than someone who is rather closed, etc.

If you want, you can also ask the participants to write down their positive qualities on the left and their less positive traits on the right. The assistant then fills in a second sheet for the person, or the participants can have somebody else do it, e.g. one of their parents, a teacher, or a sibling. The two worksheets are then given different titles: 'My personality as I see it', and 'My personality as *name of the other person or the word 'others'* see(s) it'.

Younger children and intellectually disabled people with autism will not always understand all the terms or words, or they may give them a very concrete or associative meaning. It is typical for people with autism that they do not spontaneously indicate that they have not understood something, or that they understand it differently. Checking their understanding of character traits by having them describe them, or, even better, by having them give examples is recommended.

My talents

This is an easier and less confronting worksheet than the one about nature. Here, the assistant can invite the participants to talk about their strong points, which may include special skills or abilities. In the previous session, the participants can be asked to prepare a demonstration of their skills or to bring things to illustrate them, such as a drawing, a book about their favourite subject, or a musical instrument.

This is what others find special about me

Because of their autistic thinking, people with autism look at the world differently than we do. This is also true for the way they look at themselves. This worksheet is meant to give them an idea of how other people think about them. It is meant to be taken home to have it filled in by their parents, teacher, mentor, siblings, etc. For some of the participants, it will be necessary to make a list of all the people who should be asked to contribute. This avoids the problem of having to choose as well as the risk of them asking just anybody, even complete strangers, to fill something in on this sheet. This is a very rewarding worksheet for the person with autism, certainly when he or she has low self-esteem.

My not so strong points

For some people, this can be very confronting. Some of them will try to avoid this confrontation by giving superficial answers or identifying minor, concrete weak points, such as: 'I am not that good at speaking foreign languages, but that's no problem, because I don't like going abroad anyway'.

This is what others consider to be my not so strong points

This worksheet is meant as a supplement and/or correction to the worksheet filled in by the persons with autism themselves. Once again, this offers the opportunity to point at the differences between what the persons with autism think of themselves and what others think of them. Take care not to get caught in a 'yes–no' discussion. If necessary, additional explanation can be given about seeing things from different angles and 'each person his own truth'. Denial of what others have written about them can be a consequence of a defensive attitude (often due to low self-esteem or a negative self-concept), but it can also be due to an inability to see things from a different point of view or to a lack of 'theory of mind'.

In preparation for the later sessions on autism, and if the persons who filled out this sheet didn't include them, the assistant can mention certain character-istics of autism here, but without using words such as 'autism', 'stereotyped', 'resistance to change'.

My personality: My inner self is unique

Especially for children and less able people with autism, it can be necessary to give concrete and visual illustrations to the paragraph about 'a dull world'. For example: if everyone could run or swim or ride equally fast, who would ever win a race? If everyone knew as much about the weather as the weatherman, who would ever listen to the weather forecast?

Instead of putting their signature on the bottom of the page, the participants may also simply write their name. Just as with the fingerprints, it can be fun to compare signatures or handwritings.

I am unique

A person with autism may take this statement very literally, i.e., to mean that he or she is the only one who is unique. Therefore, it is best to explain that everybody is unique!

Materials

- a pair of scissors
- glue
- a pen

Variations and suggestions for additional activities

- Have the participants describe character traits on the basis of proverbs.

- Have them symbolise character traits, e.g. by drawing animals. (But first check whether the participants have enough imagination and that they are able to make the distinction between symbols and reality!)

- An activity based on the horoscope. What is my zodiac sign? Does the description of my star sign correspond to the character traits I wrote down about myself?

- A quiz or questionnaire about the inner self and the outer self. Some examples of possible questions are:

  - John is 10 cm taller than Eric. Inner or outer self?

  - Laura likes fishing. Inner or outer self?

  - Billie is afraid of spiders. Inner or outer self?

- Have the participants make a collage about 'my inner self'.

- An individual's personality is partly defined by that person's experiences. Experiences shape a person's character, interests, knowledge, skills, abilities and shortcomings. This is an aspect which can be added to the series of character traits and the children can be asked to identify events in their life that were important to them, e.g. a trip abroad, a new school, the birth of a sibling.

My body

Objectives of this session

- To be able to name the different parts and functions of the human body.

- To know the location and the functions of the brain in the body.

- To know the way the brain functions and processes information.

- To gain an insight into the different aspects of intelligence and to be able to distinguish them in oneself.

Procedure and points of interest

In this session, it is recommended that special attention is paid to any fears or bizarre fantasies that may be aroused by the subject. The session appeals to the participants' imagination, and it is well-known that people with autism sometimes have difficulties with that and are prone to let their imagination run wild. The illustrations of the organs in particular may evoke associations with filthiness or inspire fear.

We have included only a limited number of elementary worksheets for this session. There is a wealth of interesting and valuable material on the human body that can be used for this purpose, e.g. youth encyclopaedias, children's books, and even very attractive CD-ROMs that take users on a virtual journey through the body. Moreover, all the children will be taught about the body at school. The worksheets are meant as a means of checking the readiness and accuracy of their knowledge.

My body: The outside

The participant is asked to stick the labels with the names of the various parts of the body on the corresponding places on the illustration. There is a female version and a male version of this worksheet. On the female version, the ear is not visible.

My body: The inside

The participant is asked to draw lines from the parts of the body to the correct place in the body. A medical encyclopaedia can help them to look things up if they do not recognise an organ or other part of the body. The drawings of the ear, the heart and especially difficult to recognise. This is because the proportions are not correct. It is best to point this out to the person with autism (if they have not already done so themselves, of course).

Functions of the different parts of the body

This is considerably more difficult than the previous worksheet. If necessary, the participant can look up the functions of certain organs.

My brain

Scientific research has shown that people with autism tend to be familiar with the output and input functions of the brain, but much less with its information-processing function. The process of receiving, assimilating and sending information is best illustrated with a number of concrete examples.

In view of the fact that autism is a disorder of the brain and that the brains of people with autism assimilate information in a different way from those of other people, this is a key chapter of the workbook. It is very important to check whether this part has been properly understood. If not, it will have to be repeated later.

These are the correct answers to the statements about the brain:

1: right   2: wrong   3: right   4: wrong   5: right

The answers to the questions in the box entitled 'And what is the brain doing here?' are:

I see a car coming: receiving.

I think my sister will be late today: processing.

I give the ball a hard kick: sending.

I say my name: sending.

I read a book: receiving and processing.

The answers to the tasks on the worksheet with the four drawings of the thirsty man who goes and takes something out of the fridge, are: receiving; processing (receiving+); processing; sending.

The distinction between the functions of receiving, processing and sending is not always a very clear one, because the brain carries out all three at the same time. Moreover, observation and processing are inextricably interwoven: at the moment the man sees the fridge, his perception of the image on his retina as 'a refrigerator' already constitutes an interpretation of his perception.

Types of intelligence

This worksheet is not meant to broach the subject of the consequences of autism yet, e.g. the effects of autism on social intelligence. However, it is important to give sufficient examples of the different types of intelligence. Try to avoid the participants considering these examples as items they should score on. Some children have a tendency to compare their own performance of certain tasks with such examples.

Participants of average or higher intelligence can first be asked to identify the different types of intelligence and then to give examples of them.

My intelligence

The list of types of intelligence which the participant has identified for him- or herself can also be drawn up again by another person. Once again, this can be a way for the assistant to check how the person with autism looks at him- or herself and how realistic this self-concept is.

The final remark should be given due attention. Intelligent people with autism sometimes overestimate the impact and importance of certain types of intelligence. The concept of 'common sense' requires extra explanation, and it is certainly necessary to check whether the participant sufficiently understands it. It is recommended it is explained that common sense cannot be measured.

We need our body

This worksheet forms the transition to the section on the concepts of 'illness', 'disorder' and 'disability'.

Materials

- a pair of scissors
- glue
- a pen
- a medical encyclopaedia (or a children's encyclopaedia)

Variations and suggestions for additional activities

- There are a lot of interesting and beautifully illustrated books about the human body to be found in libraries.

- There are also very attractive and informative CD-ROMs about the human body, e.g. Body Works.

- The functioning of the brain can also be illustrated with a number of mind games such as 'memory', identifying the differences between two pictures, visual illusions, drawings containing mistakes, etc.

- The section on intelligence can be added to by treating subjects such as intelligence testing, the definition of IQ and its distribution over the population (Gaussian distribution).

Being different

Objectives of this session

- To know and to be able to distinguish the concepts of 'disorder', 'illness', and 'disability'.

- To understand the term 'disability' in its relative sense, i.e. relating to the surroundings.

- To know the different types of disability.

- To get a clear view of the positive and negative aspects of a disability.

- To stop seeing a disability as an inferior trait.

- To know that a disability cannot be cured, but that there are various aids that can help to minimise the negative consequences of a disability.

- To be able to give examples of various aids and forms of support for people with disabilities.

Procedure and points of interest

From now on, the workbook becomes more confronting for the participants. Much depends on how the participant understands and interprets the meaning of 'disorder', 'disability', 'impairment' and 'restriction'.

It is hard to explain the difference between an illness, a disorder, and a disability, especially to younger children and mentally retarded participants. If necessary, the part about disorder can be omitted. If you are going to skip that part, the worksheet about illness should be followed by the worksheet explaining the differences between illness and disability. Only then can the different types of disability be explained. However, it will need to be adapted:

delete the first paragraph and the words 'due to a disorder'. You will also have to adapt the worksheet about the different types of disability (e.g., the column explaining the disorder).

Illness

The difference between curable and incurable diseases often needs some additional explanation, especially in the light of the following worksheets on the difference between a disability and an illness.

Disorder

This is a difficult part that can be left out if necessary (see above).

Disability (versus illness)

Most of the time, it is difficult to explain the difference. Certain participants will have trouble with the vagueness and relativity of the terms 'marked' and 'severe'. People with autism need to be presented with measurable, clear, and incontestable criteria and terms. This worksheet could well lead to a never-ending discussion about what is or what is not a disability or which is the most severe disability. This is natural, as there is no clear line between ability and disability.

The following explanation may help when dealing with older or more intelligent participants. 'Illness' and 'disorder' are both objective and physical concepts. They are absolute: anywhere in the world, paralysis is paralysis, no matter the person's age, skin colour, address, etc. On the other hand, 'disability' is a relative and psychological–social concept. This means that a

certain disorder may be a serious impairment in one specific context, but would not necessarily be so in another. For instance, a person who has lost three fingers on one hand will not experience any problems with certain activities (e.g. attending a meeting, taking a history class), but for others, it could be a serious disability (e.g. playing the piano, typewriting, opening certain boxes).

A disability is always the consequence of a relation between a certain disorder or restriction, the demands of the environment or the situation, and the available aids. For instance, before spectacles were invented, severe myopia was a disability, whereas it is not anymore (or much less so). The concept is so relative that one could wonder whether an autistic spectrum disorder is in fact a disability 'by definition'.

Types of disability

You may need to fill out the most common types of disability in the left column yourself, but generally a number of 'Socratic' questions will suffice to prompt the participants to name them: motor impairment, visual impairment, hearing impairment, and cognitive impairment. If the participant already knows about his or her autism, then it can be filled in as the fifth entry on the list.

The answers which the participants give in the right-hand column (identifying the corresponding part of the body that doesn't function or doesn't function well; listing the corresponding restrictions: giving examples of people) are a good indication of what they already know about autism.

Solutions and aids

Most children and youngsters with autism will need help with the table on supports and aids. It is a considerable help if the assistant presents photographs or drawings of the aids.

Some examples are shown in Table 1 overleaf.

Table I Special education and assistance	
Disability	**Supports and aids**
Physical disability	☞ Wheelchair ☞ Adapted car (gas handle) ☞ Lift mechanisms at the bed or toilet
Visual disability	☞ Braille ☞ Guide dog or stick ☞ Magnifying monitor on computer ☞ Special tiled pavement
Auditory disability	☞ Finger alphabet or other sign language ☞ Teletext subtitling on television ☞ Hearing device ☞ Vibrating alarm clock ☞ Flash-light doorbell
Intellectual disability	☞ Pictos and picto agenda ☞ Big tricycle or tandem ☞ Support with self help ☞ Adapted workstation

An adapted environment

Here too, the assistant can take an inductive or a deductive approach. The deductive method is for the assistant to name the three aspects of help and support, after which the participants give examples and write them down. With the inductive method, the assistant asks open questions, e.g. 'What kinds of things already exist to help people with a disability?' The assistant writes down whatever the participants come up with, dividing the answers into three groups on his piece of paper or on the blackboard. After that, the assistant names the three categories and the participants copy the examples on the worksheets.

An additional remark

A disability can be defined as a permanent impairment. However, for some of the participants, the assistant will have to qualify this by adding 'as long as science hasn't found a solution for the disorder'. Quite a few individuals with autism take a great interest in science and read all kinds of scientific magazines, which often carry articles on high-tech surgery such as electronic implants with which people with impaired hearing can hear normally again.

People with a disability can be talented too

In this part, you can ask the participants to give other examples. Lots of people with a disability became famous: President Franklin Roosevelt used a wheel-chair; the British Minister David Blunkett suffers from a visual impairment; Albert Einstein and John Irving had dyslexia; the composer Ludwig van Beethoven lost his hearing – and so on.

People with a disability are different

This worksheet functions as a summary and a conclusion of the section on 'being different'. To check whether the participant has understood everything, the assistant can ask a number of questions at this point, e.g. 'Can people with a disability become like people without a disability?' 'How can a disability be treated?'

Materials

° a pen

° if available, by way of illustration: all kinds of aids, e.g. a text in Braille

Variations and suggestions for additional activities

° Your local library is sure to have books about various disabilities.

° Lots of experience-oriented activities and games can be used to let children experience what a disability is like. To give a few examples:

- Blindness and visual impairment: make the participants carry out all kinds of tasks blindfolded, or wearing special glasses.
- Deafness: make them try and have a conversation wearing headphones.
- Motor impairment: have them try and walk with their feet tied together, open the door in a sitting position, write something without using their hands (holding their pencil in their mouth or between their toes), etc.
- Cognitive impairment: one of the children leaves the room while three others invent a new (non-existent) game with cards or something else. The fourth child may then come back in and join the game, but without being told the rules.

° Demonstrating how certain aids are used can be a useful concretisation. Having the children try some of them out themselves can be fun, which makes it a welcome change in this rather serious session. A few examples:

- Have the participants decipher a short text in Braille with the help of a card with the Braille alphabet.
- Set up an obstacle course and make the participants do it blindfolded and using a walking stick.
- Give the participants a sheet with the finger alphabet and make everybody transcribe their name in this simple sign language.
- Have a wheelchair race.
- Show signs in Arabic, Cyrillic or Chinese combined with pictograms, to prove that pictograms are an aid for people who do not understand (written) language.

Autism: A special disability

Objectives of this session

- To understand that autism is a brain disorder.

- To be able to name the triad of impairments that belong to autistic spectrum disorders (difficulties with communication, difficulties with social interaction, and rigidity) and to be able to give examples relating to themselves.

- To be able to explain why autism is called a disability.

- To understand that nobody can be blamed for autism and that it is caused by (as yet unknown) biological factors.

- To know the meaning of the term 'autistic spectrum' and to know that all the people with an autistic spectrum disorder are different.

- To know that an autistic spectrum disorder cannot be cured, but that there are various ways of minimising its negative effects.

- To be able to give examples of the various aids and forms of assistance for people with an autistic spectrum disorder and to be able to give examples relating to oneself.

- To have an idea of the positive and negative aspects of autism.

- To no longer see autism as something inferior, but as a form of being different.

Procedure and points of interest

Again, there are two ways of informing the participants about their autism. With the inductive approach, the assistant starts from a number of concrete things with which the person has difficulties. Next, the assistant groups them into three groups (the so-called triad), names these three areas, and then tells

71

them that anyone who experiences difficulties with these three parts has an autistic spectrum disorder. This is the bottom–top approach. With the deductive method, the assistant starts by telling the participant 'You have autism', and then explains what that means and what it consists of (the triad). Together with the participant, the assistant then identifies what it means for the participant in particular and asks the participant to give examples of difficulties he or she has experienced for each element of the triad. This is the top–bottom approach.

The workbook follows the deductive method. The reason for this is that most of the children and young people with autism these days are more or less familiar with the term 'autism' and usually know that it applies to them. However, many of them do not know the precise meaning of the term and, especially, do not understand in which way it applies to them. They sometimes deny it. For people who know their diagnosis but don't know in which specific ways the disorder affects them, the deductive method is recommended.

For participants who are not yet acquainted with the term 'autistic spectrum disorder' and are unaware of the fact that they have such a disorder, the inductive method may be preferable. This approach is often the best to use with people who doubt their diagnosis. If you use the inductive approach, it is recommended that the session is ended with the conclusion 'and all this is what is called autism' and again illustrate the term 'autistic spectrum disorder' by giving concrete examples. Moreover, you will still have to treat the aspects of causes, invisibility, spectrum, aids, and the positive and negative aspects of autism.

People with a diagnosis of Asperger Syndrome can best be given extra information about the exact place of the syndrome in the autistic spectrum from the beginning of the session. A visual illustration of the spectrum may help, but it also implies a risk of leading these participants to incorrect conclusions, such as: 'Ah, I'm on the side of normality, so I'm much less affected than the others'. (The workbook contains a special sheet to situate Asperger Syndrome.)

The same goes for other diagnoses in the autistic spectrum, such as autism-related contact disorder, atypical autism, PDD-NOS, etc.

The worksheets contain general information on autistic spectrum disorders, with space for the participant to fill out concrete examples about him/herself. The distinction is expressed visually by means of two different drawings:

about autism in general;

about autism in myself.

These sessions contain a lot of information and, for some participants, new information. People with autism are generally quickly overwhelmed when confronted with too much information at a time, and the speed at which they assimilate information is generally much slower than the speed of people without autism. This may even be true for high-functioning people with autism. The assistant must therefore take care that he does not supply too much information at once, and that he does not go too fast.

Autism (summary sheet)

Depending upon the participants' needs, knowledge, and associations related to autism, this sheet can either be handed out at the beginning of the sessions, or as a summary at the end.

If the assistant chooses to give it out at the end, the following sheet with the frequently-asked questions about autism is a good overview.

If necessary, extra explanation should be given about the use of the word 'autism'. On this sheet and on the following sheet, it is used as a general term for 'autistic spectrum' (see the above remark about diagnostic terms).

FAQ about autism

By way of addition, the assistant can ask the participant(s) to write down other questions about autism. Depending on the nature of these questions, the answers can be incorporated in the worksheets or kept for an extra question around autism at the end of the session.

Autism is the result of a brain disorder

It is not always easy to give examples relating to oneself. Making the link between one's behaviour and one's brain disorder sometimes demands a greater effort of the imagination than most people with autism can handle. The assistant may have to help. Extra explanations about how people with autism think, preferably short and very concrete, may help to clarify things.

The cause of autism

Some participants may take the notion of 'heredity' to mean 'a fault of the parents', or they may speculate about which parent passed them the hereditary defect. It is therefore recommended that the difference between cause and fault/guilt is explained. An example of a concrete illustration is the following: explain the difference between accidentally bumping into somebody (then you are the cause of the pain, but you couldn't help it, because it was an accident) and hurting somebody on purpose (then you are guilty). Emphasise that, although hereditary defects are passed on by one's parents (and further ancestors), they cannot help it. Hereditary defects cannot be transmitted on purpose.

Autism is a disability

Although this worksheet is not meant to address the triad of disorders yet, it does offer an extra opportunity to check what the participant associates with autism. To help them give examples, you may suggest that the participants turn to the earlier worksheets on which they described their weaker sides.

What is most difficult because of autism?

1. Getting on with other people.
2. Communicating with other people.
3. Thinking and acting fluently and flexibly.

People with autism notice other people's autism and shortcomings much more quickly and easily than their own. Self-reflection is difficult for them. For that reason, it may be recommended either to add more individual examples yourself, or to ask the participants to give the sheet to somebody who knows the person with autism well, e.g. a teacher, an educator or a parent, and have them add examples.

Sometimes, because of their autistic thinking, or due to their resistance against the diagnosis, some participants will see the lists with examples as a kind of score sheet: the more crosses they have marked, the more serious their autism is. It is important to stress beforehand that this is not the case. This will also be dealt with later, when they are given information on the autistic spectrum.

People with autism are different: The autistic spectrum

It may be helpful to give additional information about the term 'autistic spectrum'. A description of the autistic spectrum that uses qualitative terms (such as the different colours in the spectrum, or different positions in a room) is better than a quantitative description. However, it may be necessary to present something in a quantitative-visual way, e.g., to illustrate the different autism profiles or to indicate the difference between people who belong in this spectrum and the people who fall outside it. Certain participants may argue that everyone can encounter difficulties when dealing with others, communicating with people, or with changes. In this case, this can be visualised by graphs or bar charts which illustrate the triad or show the boundaries between autism and non-autism.

An example of such a chart is presented in Figure 1.

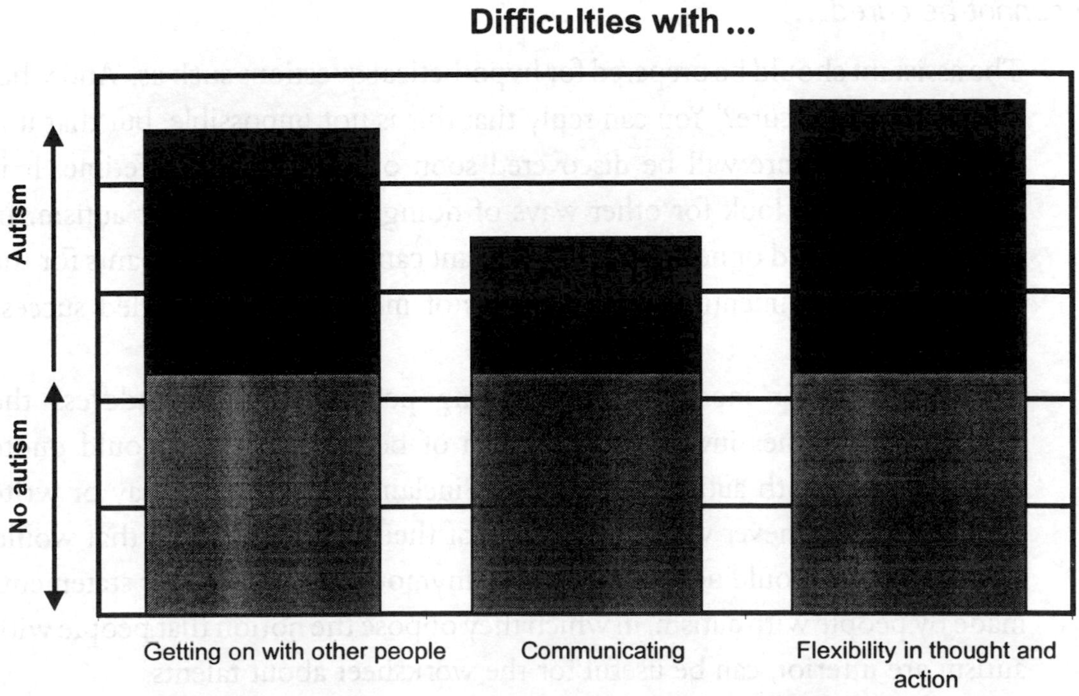

Difficulties with ...

Figure 1

If there are different versions, they are also an illustration of the diversity within the spectrum: one person with autism can deal with greater difficulties in the field of social behaviour, while another will have more trouble with communication.

Asperger Syndrome

This worksheet is meant for the participants with this diagnosis. For those who do not have Asperger Syndrome, it can be omitted.

Autism is invisible…
…but not entirely invisible

The assistant can ask the participants to give examples of situations in which other people showed a lack of understanding or in which it was an advantage for them that their autism could not be seen.

Usually, some help from the assistant will be needed to fill out the grid. Other people can be asked to give examples. The list of 'incorrect' statements about the person (crazy, silly) can be added to: 'What other incorrect statements have you heard other people make about you?', e.g. 'They say I'm stubborn'.

Autism cannot be cured…

The assistant should be prepared for hypothetical questions such as: 'And what if they do find a cure?' You can reply that this is not impossible, but that it is unlikely that a cure will be discovered soon or even in their lifetime. It is therefore best to look for other ways of doing something about autism. In addition, if desired or necessary, the assistant can warn the participants for the dangers of experimenting with all kinds of medicines or so-called success therapies.

With older or more high-functioning persons, you can address the philosophical issues involved in the idea of being cured. You could quote certain people with autism, such as Jim Sinclair, who explicitly say or write that they would never want to be cured of their autism, because that would mean that they would not be themselves anymore. Such and other statements made by people with autism, in which they oppose the notion that people with autism are inferior, can be useful for the worksheet about talents.

Still, something can be done about autism

It is important to stress that people with autism can do something about it themselves. Examples of this are an open attitude and a motivation to appeal to supervision and ask for help, plus a personal search for all kinds of aids and the will to use them. This is certainly worth mentioning to children or young people who consider their autism to be a handy excuse, as in: 'I can't help forgetting to do my homework; it's because of my autism'. An extra sheet entitled 'What I can do myself about my autism' can be added to the workbook.

People with autism have got talents too!

Sometimes, autism has its advantages. Even though this is not always easy to see and may run counter to some participants' emotional experiences of their disability, the assistant can still ask them to give examples. Their different way of thinking often result in original views.

I am special and unique

A summary sheet. If desired, the participants can make their own sheet with these conclusions and with a layout and illustrations of their own.

Right or wrong?

This question sheet enables the assistant to check whether all information has been well understood.

Variations and suggestions for additional activities

- By way of addition to the worksheets, the participants can be given a text about autism or Asperger Syndrome. Texts written by people with autism, such as Temple Grandin, Donna Williams, Gunilla Gerland, can be read and discussed. In the discussion, the person with autism can be asked to compare his own experiences with those of the author. For that purpose, the assistant may prepare a sheet with two columns: 'What do I recognise in myself?' and 'What do I not recognise in myself?' Take care that this task is not interpreted as a confirmation or a repudiation of the diagnosis: all people with autism are different from each other!

° Some intelligent young people and adults with autism will have read books about autism. This could also function as a point of contact for further discussions about their autism.

° Have the participants make a collage about the positive and negative aspects of autism.

° Ask the participants to draw cartoons about autism.

° Have the young person make a booklet in which he or she explains his or her autism to other people.

° It is recommended that an extra question round is organised at the end of the sessions, preferably a couple of weeks after the last session. We have found that people with autism may take a long time to assimilate new information, and especially if it is about such a complex and abstract subject as autism. They may, therefore, not have any questions about it until weeks afterwards. At the end of the sessions, giving them a piece of paper on which they can write down all their questions is a great help to them. In this way, the young people don't have to worry that they might lose or forget important questions. Such a sheet is also a practical means to locate and channel their questions, e.g. it will prevent them from posing their questions about autism to just anyone.

My Suggestions

....

....

....

....

....

....

....

....

....

....

....

....

....

Suggestions can be sent to:
Vlaamse Dienst Autisme
I am Special
Groot Begijnhof 14, B–9040 Gent, Belgium
Or e-mailed to:
Vda@autisme-vl.be

Part 2

The Worksheets

I AM UNIQUE!

Put a photograph of yourself here

I am unique

Contents

My personal details

Name: . . . .

Street: . . . .

City: . . . .

Telephone: . . . .

Place of birth: . . . .

Date of birth: . . . .

Name of father: . . . .

Name of mother: . . . .

Brothers/sisters (name and age):

Name	Age

My outside

All people have an outside.

The outside is what we can see.

It is called: the appearance.

I too have an appearance.
Some parts of my outside are similar to those of certain other people.

But a lot of my appearance is different from the appearance of other people.

My outside is unique.

Outer features

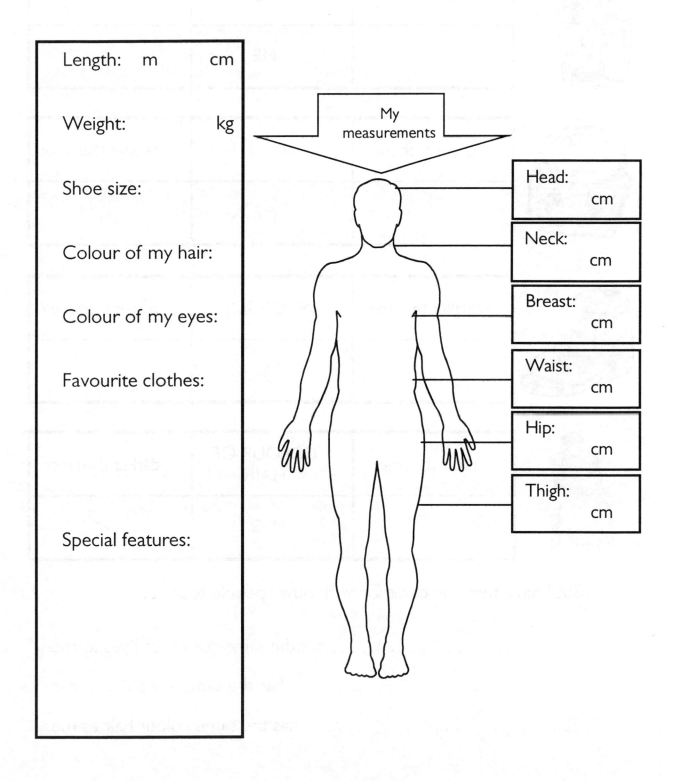

Length: m   cm

Weight: kg

Shoe size:

Colour of my hair:

Colour of my eyes:

Favourite clothes:

Special features:

My measurements

Head:
    cm

Neck:
    cm

Breast:
    cm

Waist:
    cm

Hip:
    cm

Thigh:
    cm

I look different from other people

smaller than me:	LENGTH	taller than me:
	ME	

lighter than me:	WEIGHT	heavier than me:
	ME	

smaller than me:	SHOE SIZE	bigger than me:
	ME	

paler than me:	COLOUR OF HAIR	darker than me:
	ME	

But I have things in common with other people too:

. . . . has the same colour of eyes as me.

. . . . has the same shoe size as me.

. . . . has the same colour hair as me.

My outside is unique!

All people have an outside: **their appearance**.

People sometimes look the same on the outside. You can see that in members of the same family. Then people say that they resemble each other very much, for instance that somebody has the same nose as his father. Twins often look very much like each other.

But the appearance of people can be very different too.

Luckily!

Imagine if we all looked the same…

We wouldn't know any more who is who and we would continually make mistakes…

People are always a bit similar, but very much more different!

There are no two people with exactly the same appearance.

So, everyone is unique on the outside!

You can see that in fingerprints. These are different for everyone.

My fingerprints:

These fingerprints are the
signature of my outside.
Nobody else has the same fingerprints.

My inside

People not only have an outside,
but also an inside.

That inside can also be similar to or different
from the inside of other people.

My inside consists of my inner features.

Inner features are:

- my interests and preferences, the things I like to have or do
- my character or nature, the way I relate to people, things and events
- my knowledge and skills, the things I know well or less well and the things I can do well or less well.

My interests and preferences

My favourite...

Television programme :

Food :

Country :

Book :

Music :

Sport :

My hobbies:

My character

All people have their own character, their own way of relating to people, things and events.

Some people are very calm, but other people are very active. Some people don't worry easily, but there are also people who are easily worried and anxious.

I too have a character:

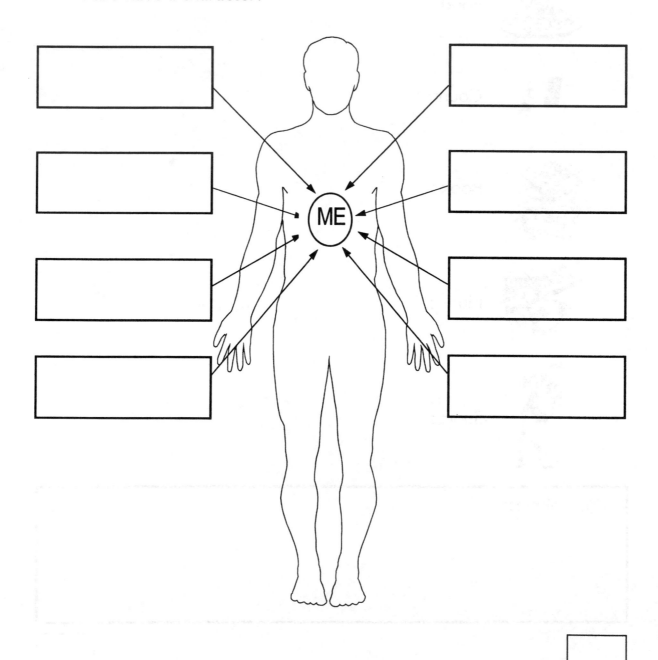

open	closed	honest
sad	happy	persevering
funny	serious	undaunted
talkative	silent	curious
active	quiet	friendly
pessimistic	optimistic	helpful
carefree	worried	sensitive
self-assured	uncertain	suspicious
compliant	stubborn	shy
cool	warm-hearted	social

My talents

Everyone has talents.

Some people are very good at music. There are people who can draw very well.

Other people are very good at dancing or sports.

Still other people have an excellent memory and they can remember a great deal.

And there are people who can speak several languages fluently. And some people know everything about animals or cars.

A talent is something that you are very good at.

I too have talents.

I am good at:

. . . .

. . . .

. . . .

. . . .

. . . .

. . . .

. . . .

. . . .

. . . .

My talents according to other people

This is what other people find special about me...

My not-so-strong points

People do not only have talents.

Not everyone is good at everything.

Some people are very good with their hands, but not so good at maths or languages.

Some people are very good with computers, but they are not very good at sports.

Alongside his or her talents, each of us also has his or her less strong sides: the things we are not so good at.

What I am not so good at, what is difficult for me:

. . . .

. . . .

. . . .

. . . .

. . . .

. . . .

. . . .

. . . .

My not-so-strong points according to other people

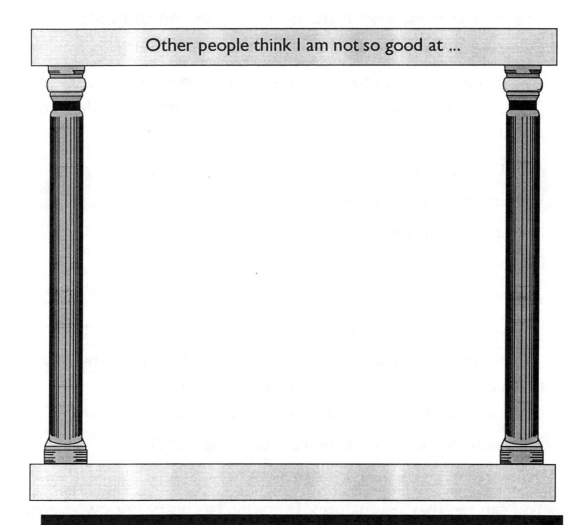

Other people think I am not so good at ...

Everybody has both talents
and not-so-strong points.

All people are good at some things but not
so good at other things.

The talents and the not-so-strong points together
form somebody's abilities.

My personality: My inside is unique!

People not only have an outside but also an inside. That inside is made up of the interests, the nature and the abilities of the person.

Together all these inner features make up the **personality**.

Everyone has a personality.

And just as for the outside, the inside or the personality of every person has some similarities and differences with the inside of other people.

And that's good.

If everyone had the same inside,

if everyone had the same personality,

if everyone had the same interests,

if everyone had the same nature,

if everyone were equally good at knowing and doing things…

…then the world would be very dull, we would have nothing to tell or teach each other, there would be no competitions,
there wouldn't be any exciting movies or books, and so on.

There are no two people with the same personality.

Even on the inside everyone is unique!

You can see that in signatures. Everyone has his or her own signature.

This is my signature:

This signature is the expression of my inside or personality.
Nobody else has the same signature.

My outside is unique!!

My inside is unique!!

I am unique!!

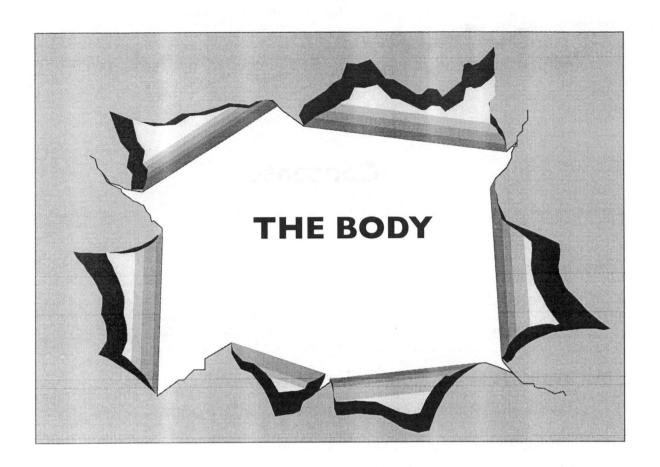

THE BODY

A journey of discovery through the body

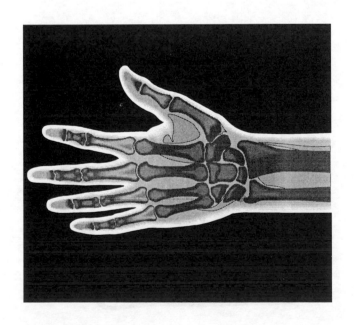

My body

Contents

My body

Just as I do, my body also has an outside and an inside.

I cannot see the inside. Yet there are some very important
body parts there, such as the brain.

My brain does a lot.

It receives, processes and sends information.

It forms my intelligence.

To perform the common activities of every day,
we need our body.
As the saying goes:
A healthy mind in a healthy body.

My body: The outside

My body has an outside. The different parts all have their own name.

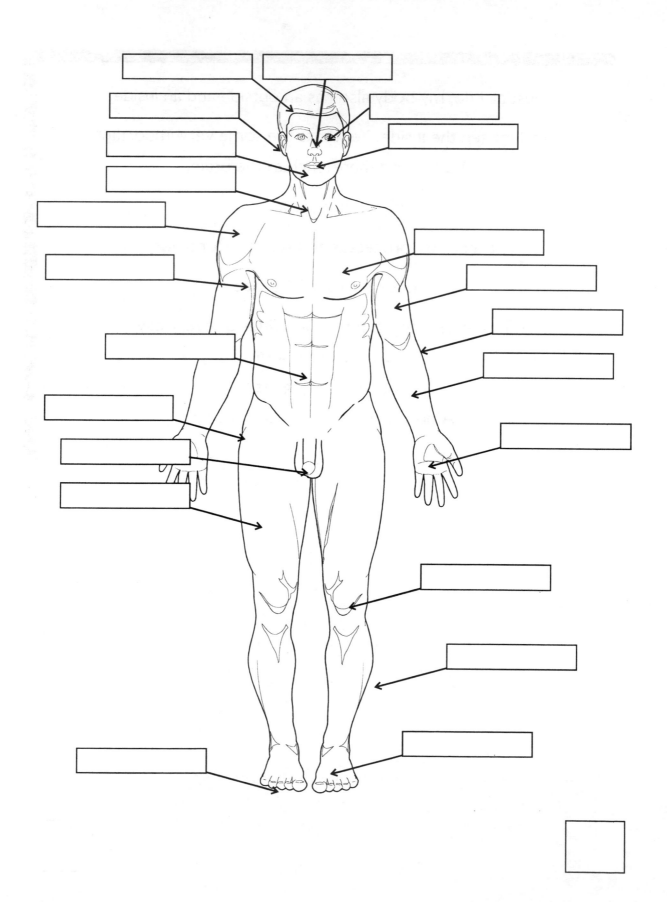

My body: The outside

My body has an outside. The different parts all have their own name.

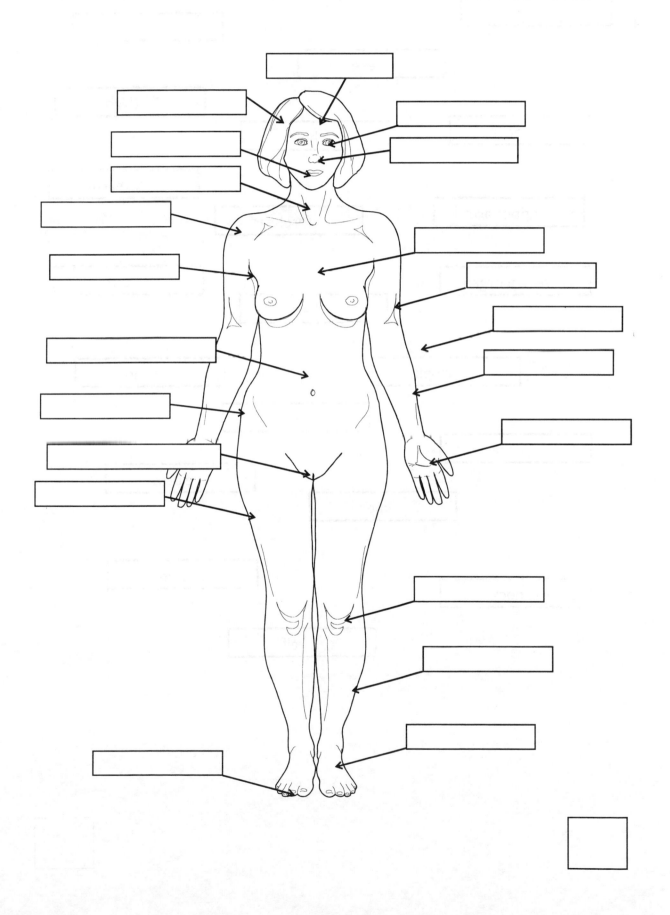

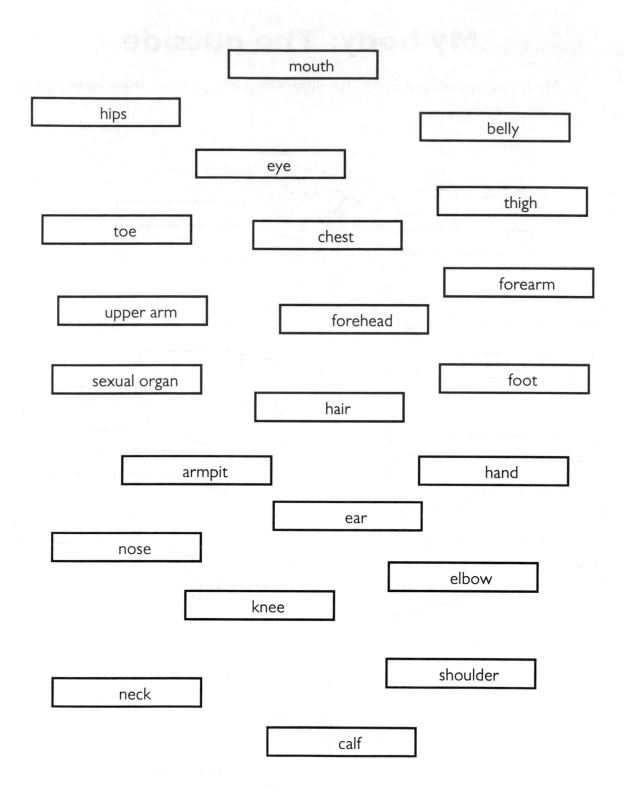

mouth

hips

belly

eye

thigh

toe

chest

forearm

upper arm

forehead

sexual organ

foot

hair

armpit

hand

ear

nose

elbow

knee

shoulder

neck

calf

My body: The inside

My body also has an inside. The different body parts all have their own place.

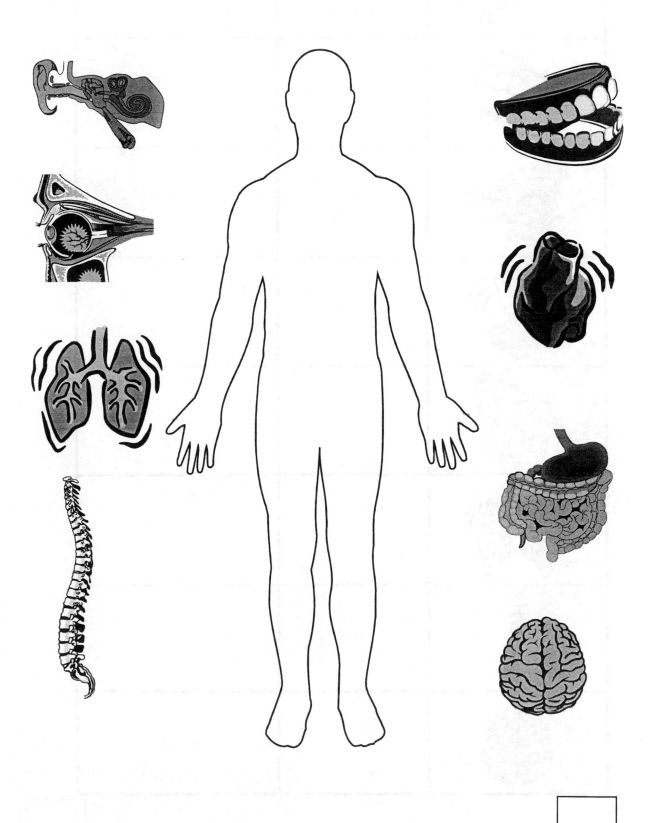

	(name) I have...	(function or task) to...

My brain

A special part of my inside

There is an important part of my body that I cannot see: my brain.

My brain is kept safely in my head, under my skull. And that's good, because my brain is very vulnerable and important. Without my brain, I cannot live.

My brain looks a little like a cauliflower or a big, slushy walnut. It is about the same size as my two fists. And it weighs roughly three pounds.

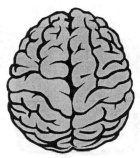

My brain is important for my body because it **arranges** everything. It makes it possible for me to:

. . . .

. . . .

. . . .

. . . .

. . . .

. . . .

. . . .

. . . .

. . . .

The brain can be compared with a **computer**. But it can do much more than even the best and fastest computer in the world. A computer that could do everything our brains can do would have to be ten thousand times bigger.

The brain is so complicated that scientists still don't know exactly how it works.

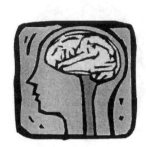

Just like a computer, the brain processes **information**. The brain <u>receives</u> information.

This means that information comes into the brain; for example what we see or what we **perceive** with our other senses.

The brain <u>processes</u> that information.
We call that **thinking**.

The brain also <u>sends</u> information.
For example: it sends signals to our muscles so that we can **move**, grab something or walk.

The signals to and from our brain travel through our **nerves**.

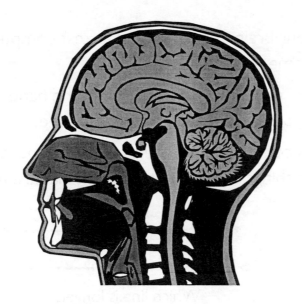

Here are some statements about the human brain.

To find the right answers you will have to use your brain!!

	Right or wrong???		
1	The nerves send messages to the brain at a speed of 360 kilometres per hour.	RIGHT	WRONG
2	The more you learn and the smarter you become, the bigger your brain becomes. Smart people have a bigger brains than stupid people.	RIGHT	WRONG
3	The brain contains twelve billion cells.	RIGHT	WRONG
4	Brain cells grow just like hair and nails.	RIGHT	WRONG
5	We only use a small part of our brain.	RIGHT	WRONG

Although our brain is the best and fastest computer in the world, it still finds some things difficult.

Try to make circles on your belly with one hand while tapping your head with your other hand at the same time!

Sometimes our brain even makes mistakes and it makes a fool of us. It shows us things that are not there or that are not correct.

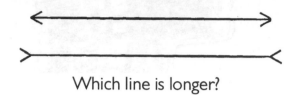

Which line is longer?

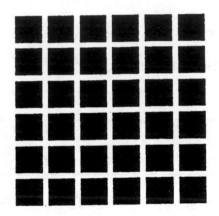

Are there really dots between these black squares or is your brain being fooled?

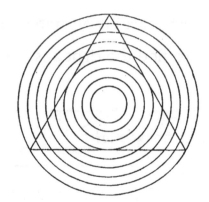

Are the lines of the triangle straight or bent?

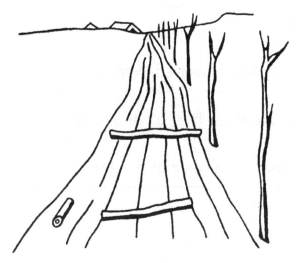

Which bough is the longest?

The brain receives, processes and sends information

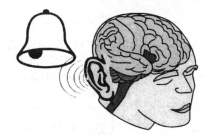

I hear the bell.
= perception of a sound
Through my ears my brain *receives* information.

RECEIVING

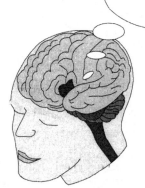

> There is somebody at the door

I think: there is somebody at the door.
My brain *processes* the information.

PROCESSING

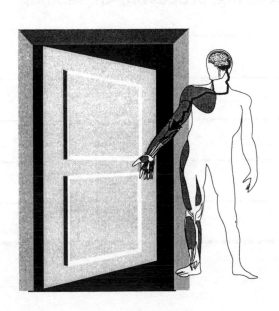

I go to the door and open it.
I do that with the muscles in my legs and arms. They received the instruction to do that from my brain.

The brain *sends* this information.

SENDING

RECEIVING	PROCESSING	SENDING
I touch something very hot.	Pain! Danger!	I pull my hand away.
I hear someone call my name.	Oh, that's me. He wants to ask me something.	I turn my head in the direction of that person and I look at him.
I have a hungry feeling in my stomach.	It is time to eat something.	I go to the kitchen and take an apple.
I see a door.	I want to go in.	I open the door.

What does the brain do here? Receiving, processing or sending information?	
I see a car coming.	
I think my sister will be late today.	
I give the ball a hard kick.	
I say my name.	
I read a book.	

Fill in what the brain does with the information: receiving, processing or sending.

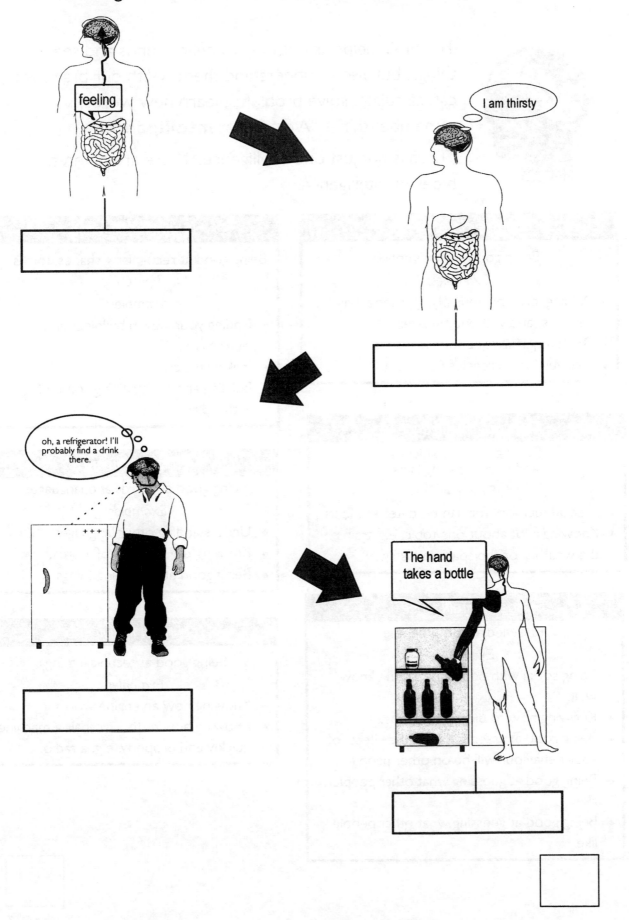

Intelligence

The brain helps us not only to hear sounds and see things, but also to understand them. With our brain, we can calculate, solve problems, learn new words, remember things. We call that **intelligence**.

There is not just one intelligence. There are different types of intelligence.

Number intelligence

Being good with numbers

Examples:

- Adding, dividing, multiplying, subtracting very fast and without mistakes.
- Remembering telephone numbers.
- Converting currencies ($ ↔ £).

Factual intelligence

Being good at collecting and remembering facts

Examples:

- A good memory for names, dates and facts.
- Knowing a lot about one topic, e.g. trains, the weather or the space industry.

Social intelligence

Knowledge about people

Examples:

- Being social with people you don't know well.
- Knowing how to please someone.
- Being good at assessing what the effects of your behaviour will be on other people.
- Being good at guessing what other people like
- Being good at guessing what other people like.

Spatial intelligence

Being good at recognising shapes, forms and patterns

Examples:

- Finding your way in buildings and cities easily.
- Making puzzles.
- Building and constructing something with a plan.

Verbal intelligence

Being good at words and languages

Examples:

- Understanding other languages.
- Knowing the meaning of words.
- Being good at explaining things.

Technical intelligence

Being good at technical things

Examples:

- Knowing how an engine works.
- Knowing how to fix or repair a machine quickly and properly, e.g. a radio.

My different kinds of intelligence

Within one person, not all the different kinds of intelligence are equally well developed.

So it may be that a person is very good at languages but that he cannot find his way around buildings and cities.

We would say that this person has high verbal intelligence, but that his spatial intelligence is not so high.

That goes for me too. Certain kinds of intelligence are better developed than others.

This is the overview of my forms of intelligence.

The intelligence with the most stars is my highest.

The intelligence with only one star is my least strong intelligence.

My intelligence:	
★★★★★★	
★★★★★	
★★★★	
★★★	
★★	
★	

Intelligence is of course very important, but it is not the most important thing. Less intelligent people may be very good at something, for example making music or athletics.

And when you have to take care of a sick person, then patience might be much more important than intelligence.

And in daily life you don't just need to be smart or intelligent, you also need common sense.

We need our bodies

To succeed in the usual activities of every day (getting up, washing myself, going to school or work, playing, relating to people), it is very important that my body works well.

For example: to get to school or work without difficulty, the following body parts have to function properly:

. . . . to walk or cycle

. . . . to see the road

. . . . to know what I have to take with me

. . . . to say that I'm leaving

. . . . to hear the traffic approaching

. . . . to carry my briefcase or satchel

Very ordinary, daily activities become difficult when a certain part of the body doesn't work well or even doesn't function at all.

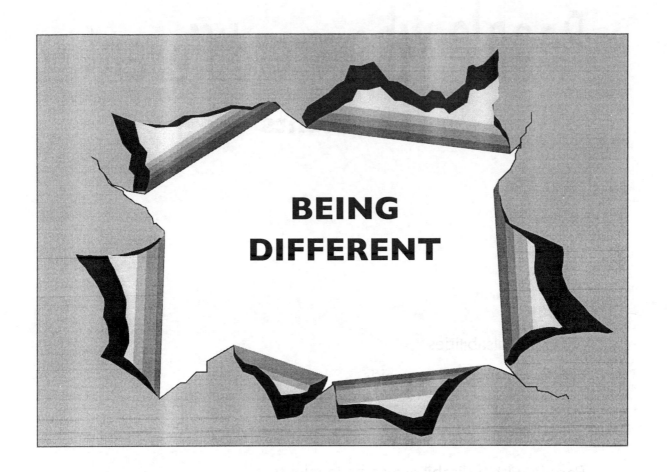

BEING DIFFERENT

About people who are different

People who are different

Contents

Disease

Our body does not work well all the time.

Then we are **ill**.

If we are ill, then a lot of things don't work that well:

- Getting up is not so easy, because you don't feel well, because you are tired or have a fever.
- Food doesn't taste that good, because sick people often don't feel like eating.
- You are not able to go to school or work: the doctor writes a note to keep you at home.
- Relating to other people doesn't work very well, because you prefer to be left alone or because you feel pain.

There are many diseases. Here are the diseases I have had:

. . . .

. . . .

. . . .

. . . .

. . . .

Happily, we are not ill all the time.

When we are ill, then we can do something about it.

We rest and we take medication. When we are very ill, we may have to go to hospital and have surgery.

All these things are called **'treatment'**.

If the treatment is good and we start it in time, then the illness disappears.

Then we are cured and we get well again.

These are the 'treatments' (medication, rest, surgery) I have had when I was ill:

. . . .

. . . .

. . . .

For certain diseases, scientists have not found the right treatment yet. For example, AIDS.

Then doctors try to control the disease or stop it getting worse with medication or other treatments.

We say that diseases such as AIDS are (at the moment) **incurable**.

For certain diseases such as cancer the treatment can only be successful when the doctors discover them in time.

Fortunately, modern medicine is so advanced that only a few diseases are still incurable. For most diseases good treatment is available.

Disorder

Sometimes a part of our body doesn't function well and can *not* be cured or treated.

Then we don't call it an illness, but a **disorder**.

You can be born with a disorder.

For example: a person who is born blind or with only one foot.

But you can also get a disorder later in life.

For example: a soldier who steps on a mine and loses a leg.

For example: a person who cannot walk any more after a car accident.

Having a disorder has **consequences**. You cannot do certain things any more.

For example:

If I had a disorder of my eyes and I could not see properly any more, what would I no longer be able to do?

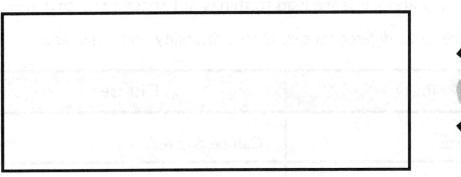

The consequences of a disorder can be more or less severe.

If you lose just your little toe, than you are not much troubled by that.

However, if you lose your big toe, then the consequences are more serious. You need that big toe to keep your balance: without it, you constantly fall over!

Some disorders have such serious consequences that a lot of very common activities become hard to do: getting up, washing yourself, working, going to school, playing.

Disability

If a disorder leads to *marked*, *severe and lasting restrictions*, then we call this a disability.

A disability is:

Experiencing difficulties and restrictions in common activities

as the result of a disorder.

A disability is not the same as a disease or an illness!

There are some *similarities*:

Both have to do with your body not working very well.

In both instances you need help, support and care.

Both a disability and a disease lead to things not succeeding that well.

But there are clear *differences* between a disability and a disease:

Disability	Disease
Cannot be treated.	Can be treated.
No cure possible.	Cure is (usually) possible.
You usually have it your whole life.	Most diseases last for a shorter or longer period, a disease is rarely lifelong.
Is never contagious.	Can be contagious.
Not everybody has a disability.	Everybody gets ill once in a while.

Different disabilities

When your eyes don't work (well) then the consequences are different from when your legs or ears don't work (well). It depends on the part of the body where the disorder is, what the consequences are.

Therefore there are different kinds of disability.

Here is my overview of the disabilities I know about:

Disability Name of the disability	Disorder Which part of the body doesn't work (well)?	Restrictions and difficulties What becomes impossible or difficult for a person with this disorder?	Who Do I know with this disability?

Solutions, supports and aids

A disease can (usually) be treated, a disability cannot.

That does not mean that nothing can be done about a disability.

People with a disability sometimes find solutions themselves for the problems and difficulties they face.

Examples:

A blind person will listen very carefully to hear (instead of seeing) who's coming. Or she will feel with her hands what's on the table instead of looking.

A deaf person will learn to watch the movements of the mouth of people who are talking very carefully in order to 'read' what they are saying. This is called 'lip reading'.

Next to that there are also supports and aids. They help people with a disability to do as many things as possible like other people.

Disability	Aids
Physical disability	
Visual disability	
Auditory disability	
Intellectual disability	

Special education and assistance

People with a disability can learn a great deal about how to do the things people without a disability do.

But a disability also has its consequences for learning:

- Ordinary school books, what the teacher writes on the blackboard, typed or printed instruction sheets... Blind pupils cannot learn much from that, because they can't see and therefore can't read those things.

- Deaf children can't learn easily from a teacher who teaches the usual way, through spoken language, because they can't hear what the teacher says.

Students with an intellectual disability also find it hard to participate in an ordinary classroom, because many things are too complicated for them, or because things go too fast for them.

If you have a disability, learning can be so difficult that you need special help. That's why there are special schools and why there are support teachers in ordinary schools.

At a special school, students with a disability learn the same things as other students (maths, history, English, etc.). But they learn it in a different way: when blind children learn about plants, they don't use photographs or pictures, but they feel and smell the plants.

At a special school, the students with a disability also learn to use aids. For example: in a school for deaf and hearing-impaired children they learn how to use sign language.

Finally, at special schools, there are also professionals who help the students with their problems. In a school for children with learning difficulties or behavioural problems, these professionals assist the students with their difficulties.

An adapted environment

People with a disability can do a lot about their disability through special education and aids.

But the environment also has to make an effort to help the people with a disability.

It is also necessary for the environment to be adapted to the person with a disability.

Example:

A person with a physical disability can learn to move around with a wheelchair, but that is not sufficient to enable them to enter buildings with a staircase at the entrance. Therefore, the entrance of many public buildings is adapted: next to the stairs, there is a platform for wheelchair users.

 A blind woman can learn to move around in the city with her stick or with a specially trained guide dog, but that is not enough for her. She still doesn't know whether the traffic lights are green or red. That is why, in many cities, the traffic lights are equipped with sound signals.

I know another example of an adaptation of the environment for people with a disability:

My example:

Although you cannot be cured from a disability, a lot can be done about it:

solutions & aids	special education & assistance	an adapted environment

But even with this support, a disability still remains a **restriction**.

Because of their disability, people with a disability will never be able to do certain things like other people. Some things remain difficult all their life. And permanent help and support from other people will be needed.

In spite of their restrictions, people with a disability can still have fun:

Some examples:

A person whose legs are paralysed will never be able to swim. (But he or she can still do a lot of other nice things in a swimming pool and thus enjoy going there.)

A deaf person will never be able to listen to music the way other people do. (But he or she can still enjoy feeling the vibrations of the music at a party.)

A blind person will never be able to read comic books. (But he or she can still enjoy listening to another person telling a good story.)

A person with an intellectual disability will never be able to drive a car. (But he or she can still go travelling around to nice places on special group trips for people with a disability.)

My examples:

. . . .

. . . .

People with a disability also have talents

People with a disability experience serious restrictions in daily life. Because of their disability they are less good at certain things.

> But... people with a disability are much more than their disability!
>
> A person *is not* a disability, but *has* a disability!

A disability is only one feature of a person. Alongside that, there are also other features.

And therefore even people with a disability have **talents**!

In other words: although people with a disability can't do some things (or not so well), they can be very good at others.

Examples:

- Some deaf people are very good at sport.
- There are people who have no arms, yet they make wonderful paintings with their feet and toes.
- There are blind people who are very good at making telephone calls.
- There are people with an intellectual disability who are excellent actors in theatre or who are very good at caring for animals.

There are even people with a disability who have become famous the world over for their talents:

- Ray Charles and Stevie Wonder, both blind, are world famous pop stars.
- Pascal Duquenne has an intellectual disability but as an actor he won a major award at the Cannes film festival.

- Stephen Hawking is completely paralysed, he can't even talk, but he is one of the most famous scientists of the twentieth century.

- Andrea Boccelli is a world famous opera singer and he is blind.

- Christopher Reeve, the actor who played Superman, has been paralysed since his accident, but he still became a successful film director.

People with a disability are different, not inferior

- Just like other people they have talents, so they can be as good as other people or even better than other people at certain things.

- There are, however, some things they are less good at than other people.

- They can do something about that: learning to use resources, asking for support, looking for solutions.

- They can also be helped if the environment is adapted

but…

…even with all this help, they can never become like people who have no disability.

People with a disability are **no less** than people without a disability.

People with a disability **are different** from people without a disability.

People with a disability **remain different** from people without a disability.

AUTISM

A special disability

Autism

Contents

 Autism

There are many people who are different.

That is because there are many disorders and disabilities.

A special disability is autism.

About one in four hundred people has autism.

Autism is the consequence of a disorder of the brain.

The brains of people with autism work differently.

People with autism think differently.

That makes them different.

On account of their autism, they experience limitations
and difficulties in common activities.

But people with autism have talents too.

People with autism are not inferior but special.

Frequently asked questions about autism

- ○ Where is this autism located?
- ○ Is autism a disability?
- ○ What causes autism?
- ○ What is different in people with autism?
- ○ Can autism be cured?
- ○ What can one do about autism?
- ○ Can other people see that you have autism?
- ○ Do people with autism also have talents?

I also have some other questions about autism:

....

....

....

....

....

....

....

Autism is the consequence of a disorder of the brain

 This means: the brains of people with autism do not function as they should.

People with autism – just like other people – are usually able to see, hear, smell, touch and taste well.

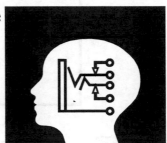

Receiving information is usually no problem.

But the information coming into the brain through the senses is not processed very well in one way or another.

It is not true that the brains of people with autism do not function. They do, but in a different way from the brains of other people. So people with autism are not foolish or stupid. But they do not understand certain things (that well). And they especially understand a lot of things in a different way.

Example:

In the classroom, the teacher tells the students to turn over their sheet. What she actually means is that the students should take the next sheet. A student with autism hears perfectly well what the teacher says (receiving the information), but understands the message quite literally (processing) and turns his sheet upside down (sending) instead of putting it aside and taking the next sheet.

Because the brains of people with autism process certain information differently, they also send different signals. That's why people with autism often react so differently from people without autism.

Autism is the consequence

of a disorder of the brain

 My example:

We do not know yet where this disorder exactly is located in the brain. We cannot point out where the disorder is to be found.

Even with the help of sophisticated machines, doctors often cannot see where things go wrong in the brain of people with autism.

The causes of autism

Usually the brain disorder is present from birth.

This means that most people with autism are born with their autism.

Scientists do a lot of research into the causes of autism but so far they have not found a single cause that occurs in *all* people with autism.

So we do not know the exact cause yet.

What we do know is that people with autism cannot help having autism. Their parents can't help it either.

Autism has a **physical origin**. That origin can be quite different, for example a hereditary disorder, problems at birth, or brain damage.

The doctors usually cannot diagnose with certainty what the exact cause of autism is in someone.

I can't help having autism.

It is not my fault.

My parents can't help my having autism either.

You can't get autism because of a bad upbringing.
So it is not the fault of my parents either.

Nobody can help my having autism.

So nobody is to blame.

Autism is a disability

 Because of their brain disorder, people with autism do not always see and understand the world as people without autism do.

That makes certain things harder for people with autism than for people without autism.

People with autism are therefore not as good at certain things as other people. For that reason autism is a **disability**.

As a consequence of their disability, people with autism experience certain restrictions in their life.

They are less successful in a number of things.

 Autism makes certain things harder for me.
Due to my autism, I am less successful than other people in certain activities.

Examples:

☺ ....

☺ ....

☺ ....

☺ ....

☺ ....

☺ ....

☺ ....

What is more difficult when you have autism
1. Relating to other people

People with autism want to belong to the community. They want to join in and do things with other people, such as talking, working, playing…

Only… these things are not very easy for people with autism.

Making friends, for example, is much harder for them. This does not mean that people with autism cannot have friends.

People with autism want to be social but being social is more difficult for them than for other people.

Below are some of my examples: what is difficult for me in relating to other people?

- ☐ I find it difficult to make friends
- ☐ Other people touching me or coming too close is unpleasant for me
- ☐ I do not always know how to react to other people
- ☐ I do not always understand why people behave the way they do
- ☐ I prefer to be alone: doing things with other people is hard for me
- ☐ When there are a lot of people around me I get restless, nervous or anxious
- ☐ I am sometimes a nuisance to other people (without intending to be)
- ☐ I sometimes make contact in a strange or unusual way
- ☐ I often do not understand very well why or when other people get angry
- ☐ ....
- ☐ ....
- ☐ ....
- ☐ ....

What is more difficult when you have autism
2. Communicating with other people

 Communication is a lot more than just talking.

Communication means: understanding other people when they express themselves.

But also: expressing myself in such a way that other people can understand me.

And that involves more than just talking.

Even people with autism who know a lot of words and who are able to talk fluently still find it difficult sometimes to understand what other people mean. It is not the language that is so difficult, but the meaning.

Example: someone can say 'nice weather today!' actually meaning that the weather is really bad and that it is raining cats and dogs. The way people look and the way they say things (i.e. their tone of voice) can give a completely different meaning to what they are saying.

People with autism themselves are also not always very well understood by other people, because they sometimes find it difficult to express what they mean.

This leads to a lot of misunderstanding.

Some examples of what I find difficult in communicating with other people are on the next page…

☐ I find it hard to start a conversation with other people

☐ Sometimes I cannot express myself very well

☐ I often talk too loudly or too quietly

☐ I do not always understand what other people mean

☐ Sometimes I take what other people say literally

☐ I get confused or excited when there is too much talking

☐ I can't listen very well

☐ I often talk about the same subject or I often repeat the same questions

☐ ....

☐ ....

☐ ....

☐ ....

What is more difficult when you have autism
3. Being flexible in thoughts and behaviour

Many people with autism do not like sudden and unpredictable changes.

They get confused, nervous or angry when certain things do not happen the way they expected or the way they thought it had to happen.

People with autism can also hold on to certain habits.

Or they (always) want certain things to be done in a certain way.

People with autism usually want to know a lot about what's going to happen. They want to know when, how long, where, why and with whom something will happen.

People with autism take great interest in certain details. Or they find them irritating.

People with autism often have one or two very special interests. They can be very engaged in these interests. And they can talk extensively about them.

On the next page are some examples of what is difficult for me in being flexible in thoughts and actions…

- ☐ I do not like sudden changes
- ☐ I stick to certain habits and routines
- ☐ I have one or two specific interests that are on my mind a lot
- ☐ I find it difficult to go to unfamiliar places or to be in unknown situations
- ☐ I am troubled by things not going the way I think or want them to go
- ☐ I suffer from certain noises or other details
- ☐ I like to know in advance what's going to happen, where, when, with whom…
- ☐ Precision and punctuality, e.g. starting or stopping in time, are very important for me
- ☐ I often do not know what to choose
- ☐ ....
- ☐ ....
- ☐ ....
- ☐ ....

People with autism are different from one another

 All people are different, not only on the outside but also on the inside. Everyone is unique (remember chapter one).

Each person with autism is also unique.

Although all people with autism share the same difficulties, they are different from one another.

That is because people with autism not only have their autism but also:

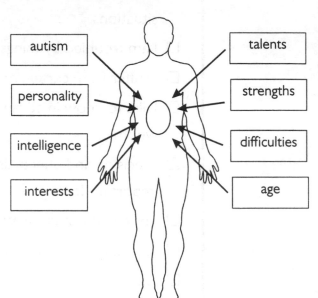

autism | talents
personality | strengths
intelligence | difficulties
interests | age

☺ their own interests

☺ a unique personality

☺ their own capabilities (talents and things they are not so good at)

People are different in all of these aspects (see above).

Some people with autism also have additional difficulties, for example, an intellectual disability. But there are also people with autism who have normal intelligence.

I do have autism but that is not the whole of me.
I also have a lot of other inner features and characteristics.

Because my inside is unique
I am different
from other people,
even other people who have autism, just like me.

A spectrum of autistic disorders

 In addition to the differences in personality, autism itself is different for each person.

All people with autism find it difficult to:

☺ Relate to other people

☺ Communicate with other people

☺ Be flexible in their thoughts and actions.

But the nature and the extent of the difficulties in these three areas are different for each person with autism.

Examples:

☺ *Some people with autism often repeat the same movements, like flapping their hands or rocking their body. But there are also people with autism who don't do this.*

☺ *Some people with autism are very interested in one subject, for instance, trains. But there are many people with autism whose main interest is completely different, such as computers. And some people with autism have several main interests.*

☺ *Some people with autism do not talk a lot. But others are voluble.*

Autism as it were has a different colour in each person. In one person it looks like red, in another like blue, in still another like green. (In a figurative sense of course! Blue, red or green people with autism do not exist!)

So there is not just one kind of autism:

It is different for each person. *The* autistic person does not exist. Each individual with autism is different and unique.

That's why we speak of an **autistic spectrum**. That is similar to the spectrum of light, as you can see it in a rainbow. In a rainbow, we can see all the different colours, but these are all light.

All people with autism have difficulties in the same three areas, but these difficulties express themselves very differently for each person.

 When I compare myself to other people with autism, I see both similarities and differences:

	Person 1	Person 2	Person 3	ME
Disability	Autism	Autism	Autism	Autism
Additional disability	Intellectual disability	None	Hearing problem	
Age	3 years	38 years	12 years	
Sociability	Withdrawn	Very active	Shy	
Intelligence	Very low	Normal	High	
Main interests	Puzzles	Electronics	Music	
Language	Does not talk	Talks a lot	Rather silent	

Even with my autism I am unique. *The* autistic person does not exist!

Autism is something on the inside. How it looks on the outside (what other people can see), is very different for each person.

Because autism looks different for each person, it makes little sense making comparisons to see who is more and who is less autistic.

Autism is different for each person, so it is different for me too!

Asperger Syndrome

 In the autistic spectrum there are different expressions of autism.

Asperger Syndrome is also a disorder in the autistic spectrum.

This form of autism was named after a paediatrician who lived in Vienna (Austria): Hans Asperger. He lived between 1906 and 1980 and in 1944 was the first person who wrote about this form of autism.

People with Asperger Syndrome, like all the other people with an autistic spectrum disorder, have difficulties with

☺ Relating to other people

☺ Communicating with other people

☺ Thinking and acting fluently and flexibly.

Hans Asperger

Some people think that Asperger Syndrome is completely different from autism. That is not true. Asperger Syndrome is a form of autism.

The diagnosis of Asperger Syndrome is usually made when the person has a normal intelligence. Professionals tend to prefer the word autism for people who also have an intellectual disability.

Asperger Syndrome is a disability too. Therefore people with Asperger Syndrome have the same right to have support, guidance and assistance as all other people with an autistic spectrum disorder.

Autism is an invisible handicap...

Take a look at a photograph of you.

Can you see on this photograph that you have autism?

No!

 As the brain is invisible, a disorder of the brain is invisible too.

Autism is something on the **inside**. You cannot see autism from people's outside. People with autism often have a very ordinary appearance, just like other people.

Other people cannot immediately see that you have autism.

There is an advantage in that, but a disadvantage too.

Autism is not immediately visible	
Advantage	**Disadvantage**
People don't treat you as a disabled person at once and therefore are less likely to patronize you or rebuke you.	Other people cannot see what is difficult for you and help you.

My autism is on my inside.

Other people cannot immediately see that I have autism.

Sometimes that's good. Sometimes there is a disadvantage in that.

But not completely invisible!

 Yet autism can be seen 'a little', certainly by people who know about autism.

Because their brain works differently, people with autism also **behave** differently.

This means:

🙂 people with autism *react* differently…

🙂 people with autism *act* differently…

🙂 people with autism *talk* differently…

> Here are some examples of how I sometimes react differently from other people:
>
> 🙂 ....
>
> 🙂 ....
>
> 🙂 ....

 For other people, people with autism sometimes come across as strange or unusual. Other people can think of your behaviour as strange and even maybe say that you are:

🙂 crazy

🙂 abnormal

🙂 ill-mannered

🙂 silly or stupid.

I am not crazy or bad!

But other people cannot always understand me and my behaviour very well. That is because they cannot see the autism in me immediately or because they do not know very much about autism.

Autism cannot be cured...

 Autism is a disability and *not a disease*.

This means that autism cannot be cured.

There is no medication that can cure you from your autism.

(Some people with autism do take medication, for example to reduce their anxiety or to calm down, but this medication does not change their autism.)

 And there is also no surgery yet that can make your brain work well again.

If you have autism, you will have it for the rest of your life.

Because autism is not an illness, it is not contagious. So you should not be afraid of infecting other people, like your brother or your sister, with your autism.

But we can do something about it!

Autism cannot be cured but that doesn't mean that nothing can be done about it at all.

Just as for the other disabilities, people with autism **can learn to cope with their difficulties** and they **can be helped** with:

✓ Special supports, resources and aids, like schedules

✓ Special education and training, like a special school or a social skills training

✓ Assistance and guidance by professionals, like a psychologist

✓ An adapted environment, like a special work corner

Below are some examples of how I am being helped:	
Supports, resources and aids	
Special education and training	
Assistance and guidance by professionals	
An adapted environment	

With special help and by their own means, people with autism can achieve a lot, for instance a nice job.

However, that requires special effort and a lot of patience.

That is because any person with autism will encounter restrictions and difficulties all their life.

People with autism remain different always.

People with autism also have talents!

 Because they think in a different way, people with autism are different from people without autism. They understand the world in a different way from people without autism.

There is a **disadvantage** in that: people with autism are not always understood by other people.

Another consequence is that people with autism sometimes find it very difficult to understand other people and situations the way most people do.

But their different style of thinking can be a **benefit** too.

People with autism have a better eye for details than people without autism.

Or some people with autism have an excellent memory for facts. And some other people with autism are much better than most people at finding and remembering the way to a certain place.

These talents can even make people with autism specialists. Autism can lead to exceptional performances. Some people with autism can excel in a certain area and even become famous:

☺ Stephen Wiltshire is a famous illustrator with autism

☺ Temple Grandin, a woman with autism, is a successful engineer

☺ Donna Williams and Gunilla Gerland are well known authors with autism

☺ Therese Joliffe has several university degrees and even does scientific research on autism

According to some authors, even some world famous people like Albert Einstein and Erik Satie (a composer) also had an autistic spectrum disorder…

Since autism is a disability, it makes several things more difficult for me than for other people.

But I have talents too! Being different from other people is not only a problem or a disability. It is much more than that!

It also makes me a bit special and exceptional.

I have autism and therefore I am…

…less good at certain things than most people

…equally good at certain things as most people

…better at certain things than most people

I am **not inferior** to people without autism.

I am **different** from people without autism.

I am **special** and **exceptional**.

I am
special
and
unique!

Right or wrong?

	Below are some statements about autism. Are they right of wrong?		
1	All people with an autistic spectrum disorder have an intellectual disability.	RIGHT	WRONG
2	Autistic spectrum disorders express themselves in an identical way in all people.	RIGHT	WRONG
3	Everyone including me can do something about my autism.	RIGHT	WRONG
4	Autistic spectrum disorders cannot yet be cured.	RIGHT	WRONG
5	You get an autistic spectrum disorder as a result of bad upbringing.	RIGHT	WRONG
6	Autism is the result of a disorder of the brain.	RIGHT	WRONG
7	People with an autistic spectrum disorder cannot make contact with other people.	RIGHT	WRONG
8	Autism is a character trait.	RIGHT	WRONG
9	About 1 in 400 people have an autistic spectrum disorder.	RIGHT	WRONG
10	Autism can be measured, so you can calculate how much autism a person has.	RIGHT	WRONG